D0194780

How to Greet the Queen
the Queen

and other questions
of modern etiquette

HOW TO GREET THE QUEEN
and other questions of modern etiquette

CAROLINE TAGGART

PAVILION

For Ros,
who understands Her Ladyship
better than anyone

An Introduction to Her Ladyship

Her Ladyship emerged from genteel obscurity in 2010 with her *Guide to the Queen's English*, in which she took readers by the hand and led them soothingly through the minefields of basic grammar, clichés and confusables. Since then she has published her views on *Running One's Home* and *The British Season*, with advice ranging from getting grass stains out of cricket whites to the unwisdom of wearing heels so high they prevent you, heaven forbid, from walking or from curtseying elegantly.

Caroline Taggart has been Her Ladyship's amanuensis since the beginning. In her own right she is also the author of the best-selling *I Used to Know That*, *The Book of English Place Names*, *The Book of London Place Names* and most recently a venture into the world of cake, *A Slice of Britain*. She is also co-author of the highly successful *My Grammar and I (or should that be 'Me'?)*.

Acknowledgements

Her Ladyship's friends are always a rich source of anecdote when she is conducting her research: special thanks this time to Lorraine, Airdre, Ana and Rebecca for their contributions, and to the various strangers on whom she has eavesdropped, particularly the badly behaved ones. Thanks also to Kristy, Peter and the team at Anova and the National Trust.

This edition published in the United Kingdom in 2014 by
Pavilion
1 Gower Street
London WC1E 6HD

Copyright © Pavilion Books 2014
Text copyright © Caroline Taggart 2014

All rights reserved. No part of this publication may be reproduced, stored in a retrieval system, or transmitted in any form or by any means, electronic, mechanical, photocopying, recording or otherwise, without the prior written permission of the copyright owner.

ISBN 978-1-907892-79-0

A CIP catalogue record for this book is available from the British Library.

10 9 8 7 6 5 4 3 2

Reproduction by Mission, Hong Kong
Printed and bound by Bookwell Ltd, Finland

www.pavilionbooks.com

Contents

INTRODUCTION

Nothing more rapidly inclines a person to go into a monastery than reading a book on etiquette. There are so many trivial ways in which it is possible to commit some social sin. QUENTIN CRISP (1908–99)

Mr Crisp's fears may be exaggerated, but there is no denying that choosing how to behave in unfamiliar situations is one of the many minefields with which modern life abounds. Etiquette has been defined as 'the customs or rules governing behaviour regarded as correct or acceptable in social life' or, more fancifully, 'the key that opens the doors to greater social happiness'. It's easy to think of it as old-fashioned at best and absurd at worst: after all, etiquette books from bygone days include such antiquated advice as what drinks to serve at afternoon whist parties ('Sherry and claret cup can be provided in addition to tea and coffee') or the correct way of raising a top hat ('The unmannerly habit of touching the hat, instead of lifting it, is an indication of sheer laziness and a lack of gallantry').

Until as recently as sixty years ago, in the days when young debutantes still made their curtsey to the reigning monarch, etiquette was drilled into the head of every child to whom it was likely to have the remotest relevance. When the time came for them to go out into the world, they would know the correct approach to every occasion, whether they were writing a letter to a friend or being presented to a visiting Ambassador. But as more and more informality has seeped into most aspects of life, so we have lost the training that produced that almost instinctive 'polite' behaviour. To a large extent, many of us would say, this doesn't matter, because we give fewer afternoon whist parties and raise fewer top hats, write fewer letters and meet fewer Ambassadors than our grandparents did. But it does mean that every now and again – when we are invited to a smart wedding, for example, or come into contact with the Royal Family – we are unsure what is expected of us. It is partly to help the nervous to cope with occasions such as this that Her Ladyship offers the advice in this book.

Mention of the Royal Family reminds her that its members are probably more carefully drilled in etiquette than anyone else in Britain today, although some of the younger element seem to be pushing back the boundaries between 'them' and 'us' and taking a more flexible approach to their own roles. Where relevant, therefore, throughout the book Her Ladyship will consider the Royal Aspect – whether traditional or modern – of dealing with a potentially awkward situation.

Etiquette is not confined to replying to invitations, arranging the glasses on the table for a ceremonial dinner and dressing appropriately for Henley Regatta. Some of the 'rules' governing these matters have remained the same for generations; they may seem to the jaundiced modern eye to have no rational explanation, except that they have always been so. But the other aspect of etiquette is the sort of simple good manners that relies on consideration of other people's wants and feelings; and this needs to adjust in order to cope with modern circumstances. It has been said that manners resemble language and fashion in that they adapt themselves effortlessly to social change; Her Ladyship would add that every now and then there comes along a social change that requires the invention of a new set of 'rules'. (The fact that the Duke of Cambridge feels able to take part in an impromptu rock concert in a way that one can hardly imagine the late Queen Elizabeth the Queen Mother doing shows that even Royal etiquette can and does change with the times.)

For example, the book quoted above on the subject of top hats was published in 1926. Its author, Lady Troubridge, although comprehensive in her coverage of the etiquette of the day, would have included no comment on a situation in which Her Ladyship found herself recently. She was queuing in the cafeteria of one of the major London art galleries. The woman two places in front of her, in the process of being served, answered her phone and began to talk animatedly. She completely ignored the young man behind the till, not even looking at him when she handed over her money. She managed to waggle a few fingers in thanks as he gave her her change, but went off with her tray without the tiniest blip in her telephone conversation.

It was a typical example of modern rudeness, though to be fair to the woman, she did begin by apologising (to her caller) for having missed a previous call. At least, Her Ladyship acknowledged, she had had the courtesy to turn her phone to silent in the gallery.

Her Ladyship was pondering this when she reached the head of the queue. Just as the same young man was taking her order, one of his colleagues appeared and started talking about what time he was finishing work that evening. Her Ladyship was served without there being a blip in that conversation either.

To Her Ladyship's way of thinking, these were both examples of staggering discourtesy. What prevented the woman from saying, 'Could you hold on a moment? I'm just getting some tea' or the young man saying to his colleague, 'Wait a second, please, I'm serving this customer'? The answer, in both cases, is lack of consideration for the other person involved, which is the simplest and most fundamental definition of bad manners.

Because there isn't always a clear line to be drawn between etiquette and manners, this book hopes to cover both. It will offer guidance on 'doing it right' on formal occasions; and it will give – sometimes opinionated, always subjective – advice on the manners that enable us all to brush along more easily with our neighbours. Her Ladyship puts forward no grandiose claims about making the world a better place, but if this book encouraged just a few of her readers to give a little thought to the comfort of those around them and to look where they were going as they walked down the street, she would feel it had served its purpose. And, because apologising in advance is a useful way of defusing awkward situations, she will acknowledge that in the course of these pages she is likely to succumb to the occasional rant.

Throughout the book Her Ladyship has used the word 'host' where earlier writers have made a distinction between 'host' and 'hostess'. She makes no apology for this. Many years ago, she attended a wedding where the groom had no male attendant but the bride's sister officiated as 'best person'; she also frequently attends dinner parties in the home of married friends where the husband does the bulk of the cooking and has long since felt that the gender specifics of much traditional etiquette are no longer relevant. That said, anyone who wishes to take her remarks as referring to one sex rather than the other is welcome (on their own head) to do so.

1

BASIC COURTESY

If a man be gracious and courteous to strangers, it shows he is a citizen of the world. FRANCIS BACON, *ESSAYS* (1625)

Good manners make the world go round a little more smoothly than it might otherwise do; they should be accorded to everyone from Her Majesty the Queen to the check-out assistant in the supermarket or the council employee who sweeps the road. The most casual observer cannot fail to observe how charmingly members of the Royal Family greet anyone to whom they are introduced or whom they meet on 'walkabouts'; Her Ladyship believes that many of Her Majesty's subjects could learn a lesson in basic manners from this behaviour.

While there is no need to grovel (to Her Majesty or anyone else), using words such as 'please', 'thank you' and 'excuse me' is likely to make people respond to you in a friendly and courteous way. Her Ladyship was recently in a small restaurant with a noticeably well-brought-up friend. The friend's chair was uncomfortably close to those on the next table. Without making the slightest fuss, she tapped the nearest diner gently on the shoulder and said, 'Excuse me, but could I ask you to move your chair just a couple of inches that way?' The adjustment was made, light-hearted apologies and thanks were exchanged and everyone resumed their meals in comfort. The incident was forgotten for the simple reason that Her Ladyship's friend had taken care not to create an incident in the first place. This considerate approach to others will see you through a surprising number of social situations.

Saying thank you

You might think it was impossible to overuse these simple
words, but even they should be employed with discretion.
Americans – and particularly American waiters – are
programmed to say, 'You're welcome' whenever anyone
thanks them for anything, which becomes surprisingly
tedious if it happens whenever a waiter refills your glass.
Bear this in mind and moderate your thanks accordingly:
thank a waiter when he puts a plate of food in front of you
or for some particular service, such as picking up a napkin
you have dropped. But don't do it every time he performs
the smallest aspect of his job.

On the other hand Her Ladyship believes that you
should always thank:

• a stranger who opens a door for you, gives way to you
  in a queue or performs any other such small courtesy

• a shop assistant at the end of your transaction

• a taxi driver

In cities not many people bother to thank bus drivers
(although Her Ladyship has observed that they do in rural
areas). But, particularly if you are leaving by the driver's
door, she recommends it as a courtesy that takes hardly a
moment and is likely to be appreciated – not least for its
rarity value.

Introductions

Tradition has it that a man is introduced to a woman and a younger person to an older one. Thus if you are performing the introduction say, 'Rachel, I don't think you've met Jonathan Black. Jonathan, this is my colleague, Rachel White.' In these egalitarian days, when first names are almost universally used among the most casual acquaintances, it is worth remembering that some of the older generation still find this unacceptable when dealing with the young. If introducing someone to such a stickler, it is perhaps best to say, 'Jeremy, this is my niece, Chloe Brown. Chloe, my neighbour Mr Green.' Mr Green is then at liberty to ask Chloe to address him as Jeremy. Or not. It is always worthwhile mentioning that the people you are introducing are your colleagues, your neighbours or your nieces, to give them a starting point for conversation (see page 80).

If a person of rank is present or the occasion has a guest of honour, other guests should be introduced to him or her. The old-fashioned idea that a single woman (assumed by virtue of her singleness to be of inferior status) should be introduced to a married one has, mercifully, fallen into oblivion, and there are now no particular rules attached to introducing two people of the same age and gender.

When introduced, make eye contact, smile, shake hands and say, 'How do you do?' There used to be protocol about who should offer to shake hands and who should wait to be asked, but this has largely gone by the board unless Royalty is involved (see box on page 16). Her Ladyship always stands up and offers her hand when being introduced to another adult, whatever their gender.

'How do you do?', by the way, is not a question. The correct answer is, 'How do you do?' And making eye contact means just that: not a challenging stare, not a coy turning away of the head, but something relaxed and friendly between those two extremes.

An aside on making eye contact

Eye contact is an important part of all social intercourse, not just when you are being introduced. Her Ladyship, giving thought to writing this book and canvassing some younger friends for examples of behaviour they considered rude, was surprised to be told, 'Someone wearing a pair of sunglasses when they're talking to you.' While she wouldn't regard this as all-encompassing rule, she does draw her readers' attention to the intimidating reflective sunglasses worn by characters in certain Quentin Tarantino films. The reason such glasses are intimidating is that they make eye contact impossible; unless the wearer needs the glasses for medical reasons, this fact makes them inappropriate in most social situations and certainly indoors. (When she says this, Her Ladyship is assuming, perhaps rashly, that none of her readers is a hit man or rapper by profession.)

Shaking hands

There was a time when ladies didn't shake hands in the sense in which Her Ladyship understands the action – they simply laid their hand in that of the person they were greeting, barely gripping at all and allowing their hand to be shaken without making any movement themselves. Perhaps they were trying to avoid impaling the other person on their rapier-like jewellery, but Her Ladyship has always felt this was an act of condescension only one removed from offering a hand to be kissed. While she has no desire to have her metacarpals crushed in a hearty wrestling hold, she believes that shaking hands is a gesture between equals; if she wants to hold something damp and unresponsive in her hand she can inspect the stock at her local fishmonger's. She also believes that some deductions about a person's character may be made

Introductions – the Royal Aspect

On being introduced to Royalty, a man should bow from the neck rather than the waist; a woman should bob a slight curtsey. The deep reverence with wide-sweeping skirt once required of debutantes is now suitable only for theatrical curtain calls. Remember, however, that it is very difficult to execute even a bob elegantly when wearing a short and/or tight skirt and, if you know a curtsey is going to be required, choose your outfit with this in mind.

It is bad form to offer to shake hands. The approach, if it comes at all, should come from the Royal personage. Be particularly careful in these circumstances to avoid a bone-crushing grip.

The Queen should be addressed in the first instance as Your Majesty, thereafter, should the conversation be prolonged, as Ma'am – pronounced 'mam', not 'marm'. Other Royals should be addressed initially as Your Royal Highness and then as Ma'am or Sir.

For more about the etiquette of entertaining Royalty, see page 108.

from the way they shake hands and has been known to take a (not entirely irrational) dislike to people whose offerings are either too limp or over-hearty.

Shaking hands is a gesture between equals; if she wants to hold something damp and unresponsive in her hand she can inspect the stock at her local fishmonger's.

Social kissing – Continental style, one kiss on each cheek, usually starting with the right – is now very widespread, particularly among women. Her Ladyship is inclined to think this should be reserved for people one knows moderately well, or, at the end of a small dinner party, as a farewell to people one has met for the first time that evening. She was surprised recently on being introduced to a group of twenty-somethings to be kissed on both cheeks by these (very English) young women. They obviously viewed it as an everyday, friendly way of saying hello and were greeting Her Ladyship as an equal. Impossible to take offence; difficult to avoid feeling that one was getting old.

Simply touching your cheek to someone else's and 'air kissing' avoids the risk of leaving lipstick smudges, but may otherwise be regarded as an empty and insincere gesture. If you don't want to kiss someone, confine yourself to shaking hands. Be aware, too, that kissing on both cheeks is less common outside London and the surrounding counties; if you do it in a remote part of Teesside you may surprise and embarrass the kissee.

Be aware, also, that different nationalities have different attitudes to greeting. What may seem light-hearted and friendly to you may be outrageously forward to a Japanese, just as American enthusiasm may seem excessive to the more reserved British. As so often in questions of manners, be guided by the other person.

Punctuality

Often described as 'the politeness of princes', being punctual is a basic piece of good manners for the non-Royal too. It is the height of discourtesy to expect other people to wait for you, as if your time were more important than theirs. It is, Her Ladyship feels, bad enough that the National Health Service takes this view of their patients without one's relations, friends and colleagues doing it too.

Punctuality is perhaps more important in the workplace than anywhere else, because lateness may (rightly) be seen as a sign of inefficiency or disrespect. Make a particular effort be punctual for meetings and interviews. If you have to travel and know that the traffic may be heavy, simply allow extra time. It is far better – and looks far more professional – to arrive 10 minutes early and have time to gather your thoughts than to arrive 10 minutes late, flustered, out of breath and out of temper.

On the social side, an invitation to a formal occasion will always specify the time you are expected to arrive. For a wedding, christening or other ceremony, this is the time when the

proceedings will begin and you should already be seated. It is a bride's prerogative to be late on her wedding day, but unpunctuality from anyone else is decidedly lax.

An invitation to a meal may specify '7pm for 7.30pm'. This means that dinner will be served at 7.30pm; you should arrive any time from 7pm onwards for a drink and the chance to mingle first. With a drinks party from, say, 6.30–8.30pm, punctuality is less important: the party will start without you if you are late and go on without you if you have to leave early. While it is perhaps over-zealous (or suggests that you are desperate for free drink) to be on the doorstep on the stroke of 6.30pm, it is also miserable for a host to be standing around in an empty room waiting for guests to arrive: the better you know the host and the smaller the party is likely to be, the more considerate it is to be

The better you know the host and the smaller the party is likely to be, the more considerate it is to be prompt.

prompt. Many hosts ask a close friend or two to make a point of arriving on the dot to help get the party underway; in a business context, the person organising the party may 'request' colleagues do the same. (Her Ladyship puts the word 'request' in inverted commas because she knows of occasions when this invitation has been more in the nature of a three-line whip.) If you tend to feel shy in large gatherings or those where you don't know many people, it is a good tactic to arrive promptly, before it becomes impractical for the host to introduce each new arrival to the guests already there. There are few things more daunting than walking into a room full of strangers who have apparently all known each other all their lives. Punctuality should help to prevent this.

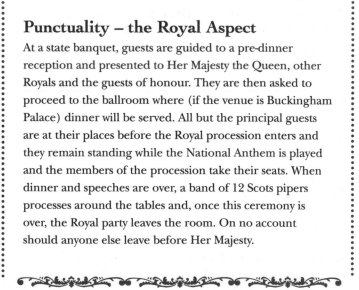

Punctuality – the Royal Aspect

At a state banquet, guests are guided to a pre-dinner reception and presented to Her Majesty the Queen, other Royals and the guests of honour. They are then asked to proceed to the ballroom where (if the venue is Buckingham Palace) dinner will be served. All but the principal guests are at their places before the Royal procession enters and they remain standing while the National Anthem is played and the members of the procession take their seats. When dinner and speeches are over, a band of 12 Scots pipers processes around the tables and, once this ceremony is over, the Royal party leaves the room. On no account should anyone else leave before Her Majesty.

If you are invited to a friend's home for anything other than an informal drinks party or 'at home', you should aim to arrive within ten minutes of the appointed time. If you are going to be later, phone and warn your hosts. *On no account arrive early without phoning first.* The italics should indicate that this is something about which Her Ladyship feels particularly strongly. Your hosts are almost certainly putting the finishing touches to themselves, the table setting or the pudding and their carefully worked-out schedule may go awry if you appear too soon. Alternatively, they may be so well organised that they are having a welcome few minutes with their feet up – and they will not enjoy the party nearly so much if you disturb them.

If you are meeting a group of friends in a restaurant or pub, punctuality matters less, but again it is courteous to warn people if you are going to be particularly late: they will find it harder to enjoy themselves if they are worried that you have been in an accident. If you are meeting only one other person – regardless of their gender or yours – being on time becomes important again: why should they sit around waiting for you? One long-standing friend of Her Ladyship, scrupulously polite in all other ways, is notoriously unpunctual. She recently hurried – late again – into a restaurant where they were meeting for lunch and asked apologetically, 'Have you ever counted up the amount of time you've sat in restaurants waiting for me over the years?' Her Ladyship hadn't and wouldn't – it would be too depressing.

Apologising

The maxim 'Never apologise, never explain' is not one that will carry you very far in social life. If you are in the wrong or have caused offence, you should apologise. If you are the offended party, you should accept the apology. Her Ladyship would be the first to admit that this is easier said than done. But it is an excellent principle to (attempt to) follow.

As a rule of thumb, the more serious the offence, the more formal should be the apology. If you have caused damage – spilling wine on a sofa or breaking a precious glass – you should offer to pay for the cleaning or a replacement. But don't let the accident ruin the evening for everyone else. Apologise at the time, return to the party, then reinforce your apology with a phone call, email or letter the next day. If the damage is covered by insurance, don't breath a sigh of relief and assume you have 'got away with it'. Send the person concerned a carefully chosen bouquet of flowers or other thoughtful present as a token of your remorse.

Make a mental note to drink less or be less clumsy next time you are in that person's company. Then forget about it. Continued self-abasement will only bring an unpleasant memory back to the surface for all concerned.

If your offence has wounded a person's feelings rather than merely damaging their property, you may be facing a more uphill struggle. In that case, Her Ladyship recommends that you give serious thought to writing a letter of apology. She had a colleague who risked losing a lifelong friend when she carelessly copied her in on an email containing a jokey but ill-judged personal remark. The friend (not unreasonably) took umbrage. A handwritten letter in which the culprit emphasised how sorry she was to have been hurtful and how much she valued the friendship eventually brought about a reconciliation. The very fact that she had gone to the trouble of writing, in this electronic, instant-messaging age, indicated to the offended friend just how serious she was.

An important note to the offended person here: once you have accepted an apology ... that is an end of the matter.

An important note to the offended person here: once you have accepted an apology (even if you have made the sinner suffer for a while first), that is an end of the matter. Try not to let it rankle and, even if you don't quite succeed in that, do not bring it up again.

If someone has offended you and doesn't seem to realise it, you are faced with several options. One is to ignore it, on the basis that they probably didn't mean it. Another is to tell them straight away that you find their remarks or behaviour annoying, patronising or whatever it may be. This risks provoking a row, but it does give the offending party the chance to put things right before they get out of hand. On no account let a grievance fester and then raise it months later. A friend of Her Ladyship was flabbergasted to be told – in September – that a cousin had objected to the way she 'took over my kitchen' when she visited for the Easter holidays. The cousin had clearly been sulking about this ever since, causing unhappiness to no one but herself and giving the (perceived) offender no opportunity to apologise or to make amends. Her Ladyship, not bothering to mince her words on this occasion, can only describe such behaviour as childish.

2

AT HOME AND AT WORK

People talk about the conscience, but it seems to me one must just bring it up to a certain point and leave it there. You can let your conscience alone if you're nice to the second housemaid.

HENRY JAMES, *THE AWKWARD AGE* (1899)

If Her Ladyship were to ask a member of the Royal Family about his or her attitude to servants, she is in no doubt as to what the reply would be: make sure they know their job, make sure they carry out their duties efficiently and treat them with unfailing consideration. Only the worst kind of *nouveaux riches* or bullies are rude to 'underlings' of any kind.

As Her Ladyship has had occasion to remark in her earlier writings, good domestic help is like gold dust and anyone with any sense will do everything in his or her power to keep an efficient and reliable cleaner (or gardener, nanny or dog-walker) happy. The old-fashioned attitude that servants should be invisible, quietly getting on with their work before the rest of the household was out of bed so that everything would be spick and span by the time the gentlemen came down for breakfast, has rightly been consigned to the dust heap (as has the notion that the ladies, being delicate creatures, were served their breakfast on a tray in their room). Her Ladyship does not advocate making bosom friends of the people you employ – it is difficult to pay a friend to clean your downstairs cloakroom and even more difficult to reprimand her if she doesn't do it to your satisfaction. But she does recommend treating the people you employ with friendly

24

courtesy and respecting the rights that they have in your relationship: the fact that a nanny, for example, lives in your house does not entitle you to intrude on her free time with demands for extra baby-sitting or help with the laundry.

Basic common sense dictates that you explain to anyone you are about to employ

It is difficult to pay a friend to clean your downstairs cloakroom and even more difficult to reprimand her if she doesn't do it to your satisfaction.

exactly what you want them to do, not least because many cleaners are novices, obliged to seek this sort of work for want of anything better. That doesn't mean you should stand over them while they make the beds, but it does mean you should be clear from the outset about anything that is particularly important to you, whether it is the arrangement of the ornaments on the mantelpiece or the way your clothes are put away after ironing.

It is foolish to distract a cleaner from her work – you aren't paying her to sit and chat. But if she is there for several hours, it is only reasonable that she should have a coffee break and you may choose to time it to coincide with yours. This gives you the opportunity to discuss any problems that may have arisen and to get to know each other a little better. Her Ladyship emphasises the words 'a little', however: she warns against telling your cleaner about your private life or, tempting though it may be, encouraging her to gossip about her other employers. If she passes on their secrets to you, she's unlikely to be discreet about yours, which could be embarrassing if she happens to work for people you know. Another advantage of sharing a coffee break is that it enables you to say, after 15 or 20 minutes, 'I must get on', thereby gently indicating to the cleaner that she should be getting on too.

While maintaining the employer/employee relationship is important, there is moderation in all things. To make coffee for yourself and your husband and sit drinking it in the kitchen while ignoring the cleaner as she works round you is taking the 'keeping a distance' attitude to extremes. Her Ladyship had one acquaintance who routinely did just that and wondered why her cleaners always left after a few weeks.

The single most important thing you can do for any domestic employee is always to have his or her money ready at the end of the day or week. Her Ladyship had another acquaintance who frequently failed to do this, on the shocking pretext that she (a wealthy 'lady of leisure') hadn't had time to go to the bank; that woman, too, found that her staff never stayed long. Presents at Christmas or on special occasions are a friendly gesture if you can be sure you are buying something the person needs or will like; otherwise, she may well prefer a cash bonus, which can be tucked discreetly into a card with a handwritten message showing your hopefully genuine appreciation.

Neighbours

Living in a flat, a semi-detached house or a suburban area where gardens adjoin brings you into close contact with people you might not have chosen as friends. When dealing with neighbours, always bear in mind that you cannot expect anyone to be totally silent at all times in his or her own home. Don't go round to complain about noisy children or piano practice unless they repeatedly reach an intolerable decibel level and/or make themselves heard at anti-social hours.

If you play loud music and entertain riotous friends every Friday and Saturday of your life, you are going to have to learn to live with neighbours who hate you.

It is only polite to warn neighbours if you are having a party, particularly if it is likely to go on into the small hours and involve late-night farewells and car-door slamming. Only the most churlish will complain if notified in advance of a birthday or anniversary, or on New Year's Eve. On the other hand, if you play loud music and entertain riotous friends every Friday and Saturday of your life, you are going to have to learn to live with neighbours who hate you. This is yet another instance when thinking of others and imagining how you would feel if the positions were reversed should guide your conduct.

Sometimes the neighbours' objection is not to noise but to smoke and smell. Barbecues are frequent areas of contention, particularly if the neighbour in question has washing on the line or wants to sit quietly in her back garden with the Sunday papers. General neighbourliness will help here: try to position your barbecue somewhere that minimises the amount of smoke wafting over the fence; use smokeless fuel; give advance warning if there are going to be lots of people; and, every now and then, invite the neighbours to join you.

It's less hospitable to invite someone to join you over a bonfire, but here again consideration and common sense will take you a long way. Don't have a fire too often, choose a day when the wind won't carry ash all over your neighbour's garden and don't leave it to rampage out of control. Calling over the fence, 'I'm thinking of having a bonfire this afternoon – do you mind?' should defuse a potentially explosive situation – provided, of course, that if the neighbour does mind you take notice of his objection: once you've asked, even if you feel he is being difficult, you can't decently ignore his views.

Be reasonable about other neighbourly sources of grievance. The deeds of your property should make it clear who is responsible for maintaining a fence: if it's you, make sure you keep it in good order.

A tree is owned and should be maintained by the person on whose property it is planted. If a neighbour's tree encroaches into your garden, you have the right to cut back the branches and roots on your side of the fence, as long as you don't put anyone's safety at risk by, for example, making the tree unstable. You also, in theory, have to give the trimmings back to the neighbour, though if you are in dispute about the whole subject this may be adding unnecessary fuel to the fire.

The right to light is more difficult to enforce: in the UK it is protected by law only if a room has enjoyed access to light for at least 20 years. You have no legal redress, therefore, if you are in a new house and your neighbour plants fast-growing Leylandii.

In any of these circumstances, it is better to have a friendly word with the neighbour and see if you can achieve a compromise rather than writing angry letters to him, the local council or your MP. Offering to share the expense of repairing a boundary fence or trimming a tree may avoid long-term ill feeling, while inviting a neighbour in for a drink on a sunny day and showing him how dark his tree has made your sitting room may have more effect than any amount of complaining.

How to complain

Whatever you are objecting to, losing your temper is never
a good idea. Unless you are arguing with a neighbour about
a tree, it is unlikely that the problem is the fault or responsibility
of the person to whom you are complaining. So while shouting
at them may make you feel better, it won't achieve anything and
won't make them inclined to go out of their way to help you.
Very often, too, anger is unnecessary. A friend of Her Ladyship
recently bought a kettle from a well-known department store.
When she went to use it for the first time it simply didn't work. A
strong-minded woman, inclined to be over-aware of her rights, she
took it back to the shop, prepared to make a fuss. The staff at the
customer service desk didn't even plug the kettle in to check the
fault – they took Her Ladyship's friend's word for it and provided a
replacement in a matter of minutes. A lot of huffing and puffing
had gone entirely to waste.

If your complaint involves something that can be put right
instantly – your food in a restaurant is cold or undercooked, for
example – quietly attract the waiter's attention and ask politely for
it to be exchanged. A good restaurant will always oblige. It is both
pointless and unfair to express your dissatisfaction *sotto voce* to your
companion but respond, 'Yes, everything's fine, thank you' to the
waiter's routine enquiry and then not leave a tip.

Even worse is to complain when it is too late for the
restaurant to do anything about the problem. Her Ladyship
recently overheard a man in a stylish gastropub tell the waitress
that his liver had been both stringy and underdone. His tone was
aggressive and she was obviously uncomfortable and embarrassed.
She offered to bring him something else and his response was, 'It's
too late now. I've eaten it.' Not, to Her Ladyship's way of thinking,
the most sensible way of expressing disappointment.

If you have bought something that doesn't work or want to complain about poor service, either visit the relevant shop or telephone customer services as soon as possible. Have the details of your complaint to hand: the date when you bought the product, how often you used it before it broke or what was said in the conversation you found unsatisfactory, ideally with the name of the person you spoke to. If you are likely to become angry or flustered (and therefore forgetful), make a list of the things you want to say.

Whether in person or over the phone, be polite but firm. If the first person you speak to can't or won't help, ask to speak to the manager or supervisor. If their response is unsatisfactory, ask for the name and address of the person at head office to whom you should write.

Don't you know who I am – the Royal Aspect

A friend of Her Ladyship tells a story of a time in the late 1980s when she worked in a theatrical agency and answered the phone to a young man who identified himself as 'Eddie Windsor from the Really Useful Theatre Company'. That young man is now known as HRH the Earl of Wessex and at the time could easily have called himself Prince Edward, but he rightly realised that his title was entirely irrelevant to both the work he was doing and to the reason for his call. Many non-Royals could learn a lesson in modesty from this fine example.

At every stage of the proceedings, decide in advance what form of redress you are willing to accept. Many firms are loth to refund money but will offer to replace the item or issue a credit note. Unless you are justifiably so fed up that you never want to deal with them again, it may be easier to accept this offer. Before you take your complaint to the next level, pause to ask yourself if what started out as a molehill is becoming a mountain. Never, ever, however disgruntled you may be and even if you are world-famous, utter the words, 'Don't you know who I am?' Your complaint should be dealt with on its merits, not because you are an arrogant bully who has a nodding acquaintance with the managing director.

Cold calls – the exceptions that prove the rule?

Anyone who spends much of the day at home will be only too aware of the nuisance of telephone calls from 'international' or 'withheld' numbers in which the caller tries to persuade you that your credit card has been misused in some far-distant country that you have never visited, that a virus has been detected on your computer or that the survey they want to conduct will take only three or four minutes. There are services which, for a surprisingly modest fee, claim to remove one's number from cold callers' lists; Her Ladyship's experience is that these services reduce the number of nuisance calls without eliminating them completely. Depending on

Now that 'hanging up' actually means pressing a button, it is far harder to slam the phone down in the satisfyingly angry way of Her Ladyship's youth.

her mood on receipt of such a call, she says either, 'I'm sorry I don't have time' or 'This is nonsense, please don't call this number again' and then hangs up firmly.

That last observation raises a sorrowful reflection on modern life, however: now that 'hanging up' actually means pressing a button, it is far harder to slam the phone down in the satisfyingly angry way of Her Ladyship's youth.

It is, of course, only fair to remember that the people who are making these cold calls are doing a thankless job because they need the money; they are not to blame for the system under which they are operating. Her Ladyship cannot, however, resist telling the tale of a friend known for her short temper and robust language who once received an unwanted sales call on a Sunday morning. She gave the caller very short shrift, using a number of single-syllable words. After she had slammed the receiver down (it was in the days when one could) the phone promptly rang again. This time it was the original caller's supervisor, wanting to know how Her Ladyship's friend dared to abuse one of her operatives in such a way. Her Ladyship leaves it to her readers' imagination to decide what sort of shrift that caller received. In general a firm advocate of restraint, she finds it difficult to censure her friend's lack of it on this occasion.

In the office

Office politics, office parties and office romances are all difficult to avoid and all, in their different ways, possible sources of awkwardness.

Her Ladyship has always found that the best way to deal with office politics is to pre-empt them by consolidating your own position. This doesn't mean toadying to your immediate superior or to anyone else who happens to be senior to you, but it does mean making sure they see the best side of you: the side that is efficient, obliging and always willing to go the extra mile. If you are regularly at your desk a few minutes before your appointed start time and not looking longingly at your watch as 5.30pm approaches, you are likely to find your boss more amenable on the rare – and they must be rare – occasions when you need a little leeway at the beginning or end of the day. On a more strategic level, a boss who perceives that you are bright and conscientious is likely to give you more interesting work to do, or to mention your name favourably to other senior colleagues. Not only will this do you good in the longer term, it should also keep you secure if someone else rocks the boat.

Consolidating your position isn't all about pleasing the boss. Her Ladyship would also advise readers to make a point of being on good terms with anyone who can make their life easier: reception, post room, IT support and the like. She once had dealings with a small company that rented offices and services from a much larger one. When the small company moved into the larger building, the managing director's PA made a point of

learning the names of everyone in reception and in the post
room, and getting on good terms with them – something few
of the existing residents of the building had bothered to do.
Thereafter, in a system in which the post was scheduled to leave
the building at 4pm, she was frequently heard begging for a few
minutes' grace while she addressed an urgent package – and
because she had made the effort to be friendly, they were
generally willing to do her a favour.

To sum up, therefore, Her Ladyship would advise being
courteous to everyone (she hopes that goes without saying), but
taking particular care of those whose goodwill can help you and,
perhaps even more importantly, whose ill will can make your life
a complete misery.

Dressing the part

Fitting in with the company ethos is another important way of
ensuring general goodwill. The most obvious example of this is
dress code: at an interview, you cannot go wrong dressing smartly,
but thereafter you should take your lead from your peers. While
a classic suit (for both sexes) may be expected in a bank or
solicitor's office, in an advertising agency you can afford to be –
and indeed may be encouraged to be – more flamboyant. A word
of warning to women,
however: unless you are
employed in a strip club,
you should strictly curtail
the amount of bust, leg

*If ever you find yourself wondering,
'Is that a bit revealing?', assume
that it is and wear something else.*

or midriff you display at work. If ever you find yourself wondering,
'Is that a bit revealing?', assume that it is and wear something else.

Even if the dress code is casual and you routinely go to work
in jeans and a tee-shirt, Her Ladyship's advice is that you smarten
up whenever you are meeting clients or representing the company

to the public. First impressions are always important, and a potential client may well assume that someone who is slipshod about their clothes is likely to be lackadaisical about business too.

Dress is only one example of company ethos, but the rules of dress can be adapted to apply to general behaviour. If the atmosphere is subdued and conventional, a brash conversational style and risqué jokes will not go down well. There are many companies in which your prospects will be limited if you don't 'fit in', if you aren't quite 'one of us' – no matter how efficient your work is. You may deplore this in principle as much as you like; in practice, Her Ladyship ventures to suggest, if you want to succeed in that milieu, you have to conform to it.

Office parties

The important thing to remember at an office party is that you are still at work. This remains true even if you have all gone out to a pub or a hired venue. Your boss is still your boss and you have to face your colleagues the next day. Drinking copious quantities of free wine and telling your boss what you think about your annual bonus or his or her management style may seem like a good idea at the time. But – and Her Ladyship speaks from a wide experience here – you are going to regret it in the morning and possibly for several mornings thereafter.

Her Ladyship speaks from a wide experience here – you are going to regret it in the morning and possibly for several mornings thereafter.

The remorse is even more painful if the party takes place on a Friday. A friend of Her Ladyship remembers many years ago over-indulging at a colleague's leaving party on a Friday night. She spent the weekend in an agony of mortification, not sure what she had said to whom and dreading facing her boss on Monday morning. In fact the boss, a hard drinker himself, said simply, 'That was a good night on Friday. Did you get home all right?' But it didn't recover the lost weekend. Imagine committing a similar indiscretion at the office Christmas party and not going back to work for nearly a fortnight. Her Ladyship cannot stress too strongly that moderation is the only sensible course here.

Office romances

As for office romances, it is easy to say, 'Don't do it' but impossible to ignore the fact that doctors frequently marry doctors and lawyers marry lawyers: in adult life, the easiest way to meet anyone with whom you are likely to have something in common is at work. Her Ladyship therefore offers these few guidelines:

• At the start of any relationship, be discreet. Don't have lunch together more often than with other colleagues; if you go for a drink after work, don't choose the office local; and don't hold hands, put your heads together or give off other obvious signals in the workplace.

• If the relationship proves to be serious, tell people, particularly the bosses of both parties, before what began as mild speculation becomes common currency. However circumspect you have been, your colleagues probably know (or think they know) and will appreciate being told the truth.

• Do not accord your loved one special treatment. This is particularly important if one of you is in a senior position. The junior should still come in on time, perform his or her share of unpopular tasks and not expect or gain access to confidential information that he or she would not otherwise have. Someone who is going out with the boss is bound to inspire some ill feeling: you should both make sure that any resentment is clearly groundless.

- If the relationship breaks up, don't let feelings spill over into the office. You have treated your partner with professional respect all the time you were together; you should treat your ex in exactly the same way.

- If you cannot follow these guidelines, one of you should leave. Drastic but true: conflicts of interest during a relationship or uncontrollable resentment afterwards have no place in the working environment.

Communications within the office

Most communications between colleagues, or between the boss and members of his or her staff, should be either face to face or by email. The speed and efficiency of email make it ideal for routine matters. However, bad news should always be given face to face; using electronic means to dismiss anyone, inform them they have been passed over for promotion or rebuke them for poor performance is cowardly as well as rude.

If face to face is not possible, always use the telephone to handle a difficult conversation or negotiation: this is a matter not so much of courtesy as of tactics. It is much easier to get your message across if you can use the subtleties of tone of voice that are by definition absent from email; you should also be able tell whether the other person is confident or diffident, angry or hurt, making a stand on a matter of principle or just making a fuss. A colleague of Her Ladyship once received what read like an angry email from a client intimating that all the work of the last week was unsatisfactory and would have to be done again. One soothing phone call made it clear that the client was not so much angry as

confused. Once the rationale was explained to him he was happy to go along with the proposal; and in the end he was delighted with the results. An exchange of emails, with their tone misinterpreted as the initial one's had been and giving little scope for gentle persuasion, would have taken much longer to achieve the same result, and might easily have failed altogether.

Here is a further example, indicative as much of the dangers of the generation gap as of anything else. A friend of Her Ladyship, about to go to a meeting that would take her out of the office for the rest of the day, asked her (much younger) assistant to ring a contractor to make sure that the project he was due to finish that week was on time. Back in the office the following morning, she asked her assistant if she had spoken to the man in question.

'Well,' came the reply, 'I emailed him and he said everything was fine, but he was quite grumpy.'

Her Ladyship and the assistant both knew that the contractor had a tendency to grumpiness. But had the younger woman used the phone, she would have been able to say, 'Just ringing to see that everything's OK' in a positive, friendly tone and been in a position to soothe the first sign of ruffled feathers. Using email gave this touchy man the opportunity to feel that he was being checked up on – and to take offence.

Texting is generally inappropriate in the office and should never be used for bad news. Stories of celebrities who dump their partners by text indicate an insensitivity beyond most people's wildest imaginings; Her Ladyship would say the same of anyone who used a text to dismiss anyone. She is also of the view that texting your boss is unacceptably casual, unless it is in response to a text from him or her. Be warned, too, that if you text rather than phone in sick, people will assume it is to hide how healthy you sound and be considerably less than sympathetic the next time you put in an appearance.

For more on modern means of communication, see Chapter 11 (page 140).

3

OUT AND ABOUT

Great things are done when men and mountains meet;
This is not done by jostling in the street.

WILLIAM BLAKE, GNOMIC VERSES (C. 1800)

As Her Ladyship mentioned in Chapter 1, the Royal Family on walkabout is an example to us all on how to behave to chance-met people in the street. True, most of the people the Royals meet are held at bay by crash barriers or at least carefully arranged to form an orderly queue, but it is hard to imagine Her Majesty or any of Their Royal Highnesses bumping into a stranger because they weren't looking where they were going.

The ubiquity of the mobile phone and the obsessive need many people have to check their Twitter feed at every opportunity has created a new curse, particularly for city dwellers: the feeling that almost everywhere you go someone is about to walk into you (or walk under a car) because they are looking at the tiny screen in their hand rather than paying attention to where they are going. Her Ladyship often feels as if her fellow street-users are playing some new twist on the adolescent game of 'chicken' – seeing

> *Her Ladyship realises that her words on this subject are likely to fall on deaf ears, but she is still going to write them: 'This is rude. Don't do it.'*

how close they can approach a passer-by before acknowledging his or her existence and moving out of the way. The rule seems to be, 'Move when you see their feet', but this brings the Twitter-checker or text-sender into uncomfortable proximity with almost every pedestrian they meet. Her Ladyship realises that her words on this subject are likely to fall on deaf ears, but she is still going to write them: 'This is rude. Don't do it.'

To those who have just shrugged their shoulders and carried on, she will add, 'If you have no respect for other people, at least have some concern for your own survival.' At a busy road junction near where Her Ladyship lives, she frequently hears cars screeching to a halt because these screen-fixated pedestrians are crossing against the lights without so much as a glance to right or left.

The invention of the suitcase-on-wheels has added another hazard to walking down the street. Where once one had simply to beware of old ladies with shopping trolleys, now a vastly increased number of people have appendages of whose size, scope and movement they seem unaware. While Her Ladyship is a great advocate of the sort of suitcase that reduces strain on the carrier's back and shoulders, she does urge her readers to remember that these devices take up space and have sharp corners: be careful if you are pulling one while trying to nip between groups of people in a crowded street.

She must also here confess to a pet aversion: umbrellas. Her Ladyship has never quite understood how the spokes of every umbrella, whether carried by a companion or by a passing stranger, whatever their height, manage to be at eye level. While she admits that in heavy rain one is inclined to hunch over, look at the ground to avoid walking in puddles and hurry to reach the shelter of one's destination, she would also ask umbrella-users to realise that they are carrying a lethal weapon and, again, to attempt not to assault those around them.

Don't just stand there – a checklist

Some years ago there was a vogue for car stickers, often displayed on powerful Volvos or BMWs, that said, 'Yes, I do own the road.' Observing the inconsiderate way that many people behave in public, Her Ladyship (perhaps growing less tolerant as the years go by) wonders if there might be a market for tee-shirts or backpacks that boast, 'Yes, I do own the pavement/doorway/ aisle.' Feeling, however, that too few people would appreciate the self-mocking humour, she has instead compiled a checklist of places where it is courteous to be aware of the existence of others. It is by no means exhaustive; it is merely inspired by the places where she has recently been irritated by the thoughtlessness of her fellow human beings.

- **In a supermarket**, don't park your trolley in the middle of an aisle or yourself in front of a shelf so that it is impossible for anyone else to reach the products on it. By all means take your time to decide which flavour of yoghurt or brand of washing powder you want, but make way for other, more decisive people to help themselves. At the checkout, have your purse or credit card ready: don't wait until you reach the front of the queue to rummage for your wallet at the bottom of an enormous bag, as if the fact that you have to pay for your purchases has come as a surprise.

- **In a doorway**, at the top or bottom of an escalator or staircase, by the entrance to a Tube station or anywhere else where people are coming and going: even if you have just bumped into a long-lost friend, move out of the way before embarking on a lengthy chat.

- **At a bus stop:** you may not want this bus, but other people do. Stand back and let them board.

- **In the middle of the pavement:** if you have to stop – to rearrange heavy bags, find your keys or look at a map – move to one side.

- **At a crowded bar:** once you have been served, move away and let others in.

- **If you are waiting to board a train or Tube**, do what the common-sense announcements ask you to do: let those alighting off first. The train is unlikely to go without you and a few seconds of patience will avoid much pushing and jostling.

Her Ladyship is sure none of her readers would dream of transgressing in any of these areas, but nonetheless she feels better for having got this little rant off her chest.

ATM etiquette

Cash machines always advise users to hide their PIN (or, increasingly and to Her Ladyship's unfailing annoyance, their PIN number – what *do* people think the N stands for?). In an ideal world, shielding your PIN should not be necessary, because a courteous person would keep their distance while waiting behind you. There is an invisible but discernible line between standing close enough to maintain your place in a queue and standing just that little bit *too* close.

This phenomenon is also noticeable in conversation: someone who 'invades your space' by standing too close makes you feel uncomfortable, because they seem to be forcing you into an unwelcome intimacy. Her Ladyship advises against this, too; the difference being that if you stand too close to someone at a party or in the office, whatever other impressions you may give, you are unlikely to be mistaken for a mugger.

'On the train'

The triple horrors of modern travel are other people's music, other people's backpacks and other people's mobile-telephone conversations. Mobile etiquette is complicated enough to deserve a section to itself (see page 47). As for the first two, Her Ladyship's advice is simple, if, perhaps, in danger of becoming repetitive: consider other people. Turn the music down so that the rest of the carriage is not treated to that peculiarly irritating buzz that

In the street

Tradition has it that a gentleman walks on the outside
of the pavement, to protect a lady from splashes,
marauders and other nuisances. Most people nowadays
think this is unnecessary, but Her Ladyship retains a
sentimental attachment to it. Two gentle pieces of
advice, therefore:

• If you are the man and want to move to the outside, do
it deftly and unobtrusively, without pushing or nudging
your companion. A piece of gallantry ceases to be gallant
if you make a song and dance about it.

• If you are the woman and a man chooses to walk between
you and the kerb, let him. There's no need to say thank
you or even to acknowledge the gesture, but it would be
rude to object or, worse, to laugh at him.

emanates from many headphones; be aware, if you are wearing
a backpack, that your usual body shape has been considerably
extended. On a crowded train or bus, take your pack off and put
it on the floor in front of you or on your lap. That way you won't
inadvertently bang the head or midriff of the unoffending person
sitting or standing next to you. If the vehicle isn't crowded, by all
means put your pack on the seat beside you, but be ready to move
it the moment more people board. Don't wait to be asked or for an
approaching passenger to give you a pointed, disapproving look.

Seats

So-called 'priority seats' on some forms of public transport specify that they are for the elderly, the disabled, pregnant women or those carrying children or heavy shopping. Others content themselves with saying, 'Please offer this seat to anyone less able to stand than you' and this latter request is all the advice you need. If you are capable of standing and you see someone who is struggling, offer them your seat.

This rule applies regardless of your gender or theirs. Stand up first so that they know you mean it. Then tap them on the shoulder if necessary, smile and say, 'Would you like to sit down?' No further conversation is required, but if they accept or refuse politely, acknowledge their thanks. If they are rude enough to take offence, ignore them and feel free to sit down again.

If you are offered a seat, whether you choose to accept it or not, be civil. Even if every fibre of your feminist being is offended, remember that the person doing the offering is being courteous according to his or her lights. By all means say, 'No, I'm fine, thank you' or 'I'm not going far', but say it pleasantly. If you accept the offer, of course, you should do that pleasantly too.

If you are offered a seat, whether you choose to accept it or not, be civil.

If, by any chance, you genuinely need to sit down and no one is offering – if you are pregnant but not yet visibly so, for example – it is perfectly acceptable to ask someone sitting near you to give up their seat. A simple explanation such as 'I'm pregnant and I don't feel very well' should prompt someone within earshot to come to your rescue. (There's no need for more medical detail than that: no one wants to hear about your morning sickness, particularly not strangers on the bus.) Her Ladyship has one young friend who, in the early stages of pregnancy, wore a 'baby on board' badge when she was going on public transport. She wouldn't have dreamed of wearing it at any other time, but it was summer and she had become unusually susceptible to heat. Another, older friend carried a walking stick for a few weeks after she had had minor surgery – not necessarily because she needed it but because it alerted other people to her potential vulnerability. Both sensible precautions, in Her Ladyship's view.

Opening doors

Having a door held open for you is much like being offered a seat: you should thank the person concerned, whether it is a stranger or a companion. Men of a certain age still believe it is courteous to hold a door open for any woman; Her Ladyship thinks that the courtesy should be extended to anyone of either sex who, for reasons of age, infirmity or being laden with luggage, would find it hard to open the door themselves. In fact, it is rude to let a door shut in anyone's face. It is also rude to make a fuss if you feel that a man opening a door for you is patronising. Just go through it in front of him and say thank you.

The mobile

Her Ladyship gave in the Introduction the example of a woman who was too busy talking on her phone to be polite to the person selling her tea. She was also recently at a theatre where the woman seated in front of her kept her Blackberry turned on and checked it throughout the performance. The production was a particularly popular one, at the time the 'hottest ticket in town' and the woman probably paid at least £50 for her seat. Her Ladyship couldn't understand why, at that price, she didn't watch the play. Her behaviour was immensely distracting to everyone seated nearby.

We are all, sadly, inured to the banal 'I'm on the train' monologues without which no railway journey seems to be complete. Her Ladyship was intrigued to discover that a variation on this theme had caused concern to etiquette experts at least three-quarters of a century before the advent of the mobile phone.

Etiquette and the arts

In addition to checking a phone (see page 47), there are many pieces of antisocial behaviour that Her Ladyship would urge readers to avoid in theatres, cinemas, art galleries and heritage locations.

- Don't wear a tall or broad-brimmed hat anywhere that it might impede someone else's view.

- Remember that, at a live performance, the stage and auditorium form part of the same room: if you can hear the actors or musicians, it's likely that they can hear you. Don't talk, even in whispers, and don't rustle sweet wrappers either.

- Be considerate, too, of other members of the audience: even in a cinema or somewhere else where the performance is not 'live', don't fidget, crunch popcorn or slurp drinks.

- In the cinema, stop talking once the credits begin and don't talk until they roll at the end.

Lady Troubridge, writing in the 1920s, observed:

It should be remembered that the railway train is a public place, and therefore it is not correct to discuss family affairs or talk loudly about mutual friends or acquaintances. The habit of talking about other people in public is most uncivil.

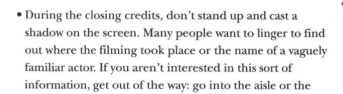

- During the closing credits, don't stand up and cast a shadow on the screen. Many people want to linger to find out where the filming took place or the name of a vaguely familiar actor. If you aren't interested in this sort of information, get out of the way: go into the aisle or the foyer to put your coat on.

- In a museum or art gallery, be aware that everyone wants to look at the exhibits and read the captions. Don't linger in such a way as to exclude others. On the other hand, don't push in in front of someone who is clearly engrossed. If you are too impatient to wait your turn, go and look at something else, then come back when the coast is clearer.

- If at all possible, leave prams and pushchairs at home or in the cloakroom. Their occupants are almost certainly too young to appreciate the art, and the paraphernalia that necessarily accompanies them takes up a lot of space in a crowded gallery. Her Ladyship would take this point further and say that she finds it peculiarly irritating to be forced to make way for an empty pushchair whose small passenger is being carried in a parent's arms.

Returning to the twenty-first century, Her Ladyship recently overheard a young woman arguing with her mother over the phone on a crowded bus. The point at issue was a pair of white shoes in which the girl was not going to be seen dead and the conversation included the line, 'I don't know what sort of nightclubs you go to, Mum, but the nightclubs I go to…' The sentence trailed off into indignation which no words could convey. Although it undeniably amused a number of the passengers sitting nearby, Her Ladyship feels that this sort of conversation should not be held in a public place.

While it would clearly be absurd to attempt to ban the use of phones in public, there are perhaps a few general rules that can be extrapolated from these examples:

- As ever, be considerate of others. Never hold a conversation loud enough to disturb fellow passengers.

- Never conduct an argument or an intimate conversation where it can be overheard.

- More as a matter of common sense than of courtesy, never give out credit card details, financial information or anything else that might be considered a security risk.

- Never use your phone in a quiet carriage or anywhere that others might expect a reasonable amount of peace and quiet. In an art gallery or museum, a place of worship, a stately home or a library, turn it off, or at least put it on silent. You *can* be out of touch for an hour or so, really you can.

- In a restaurant, take into account the views of the person you are with. The young seem to consider it perfectly acceptable to carry on their online activities while out with friends. The older

The young seem to consider it perfectly acceptable to carry on their online activities while out with friends. The older generation does not. generation does not. As a friend of Her Ladyship, in her sixties, said to her high-flying thirty-something son, 'Are you having supper with me or are you still at work?' Had the son been out with his peers, such a question would have been irrelevant; as it was, he quite rightly apologised and put the phone away.

- If you *have* to keep your phone on in a social situation because you are expecting a genuinely important call, explain the circumstances to your companion(s) as soon as you meet them and leave the phone on the table in front of you. Don't take other calls or check other messages. If the critical call comes, excuse yourself and take it in private. Then turn the phone off and put it away.

A note about photography

As with telephone conversations, so with photographs – there is a time and a place. You may be desperate to record the fact that you are within snapping distance of the Houses of Parliament or the Eiffel Tower; others may be trying to get to work or cramming some urgent shopping into their lunch hour. You are (presumably) on holiday; you have all day. Move out of the way of those who do not. Apart from anything else, you are less likely to be jostled while taking the photo if you are out of the main thoroughfare.

Breast-feeding

Times change, and etiquette must change with them. The question of breast-feeding in public would never have appeared in a 1920s guide; even the 1990s *Debrett's New Guide to Etiquette and Modern Manners* remarked that it is 'bad manners to expel any liquid from any orifice in public, and breast-feeding is no

The question of breast-feeding in public would never have appeared in a 1920s guide.

different'. Nowadays, most young mothers would feel rather differently and rightly resent being branded as strident feminists for discreetly feeding their babies when the need arises.

Her Ladyship would emphasise the word 'discreetly', however, and advises any mother whose baby is likely to need feeding to ask the owner of a restaurant, café, shop or gallery if there is a quiet corner where she may sit. She should also be aware of the likely views of her company. As a young friend of Her Ladyship, the mother of a two-month-old daughter, put it, 'It's all very well in front of my friends who have babies, because they're all doing it. But my father-in-law would be a different matter. And to be honest, if I felt I was embarrassing someone, I'd be embarrassed too.'

This particular friend got round the problem by tucking her baby under a purpose-designed cape-cum-pinafore. A gap around the neck meant that the mother could see the child and the child could see the mother, but no one else could have seen there was a baby under there, never mind a breast.

It seemed to Her Ladyship the perfect solution: mother and baby were entirely content, and no one was made to feel in any way uncomfortable.

On the road

Losing your temper when you're behind the wheel is both futile and dangerous. One friend of Her Ladyship, a keen gardener, keeps lavender in the footwell of his car in order to fend off stress. The action of his feet as he drives crushes it and releases the soothing aroma familiar from relaxing bubble baths.

This approach wouldn't suit anyone suffering from hay fever, but might otherwise be an appealing alternative to gentle music or the soft buzz of radio conversation. Beware of controversial radio programmes: if you are easily provoked to anger, spokespeople who don't share your views on the issues of the day can be just as accident-inducing as fellow road users.

Keeping a hold on your own temper is one way of promoting safer driving; equally important is avoiding causing annoyance to others who may not be as firmly in control of their emotions as you are. So bear in mind these pointers:

• Keep a safe distance from the car in front. Its dithering driver may find the side street he is looking for and turn without warning; or he may have to brake suddenly. If you hit him from behind, however slowly and irritatingly he may have been moving, you were too close.

• Use your indicators, even if you think it is obvious what you are doing. There may not be a car behind you, but a pedestrian in front may mistakenly think it is safe to cross if you don't indicate.

• Don't sound your horn except in an emergency. Beeping to indicate annoyance in a traffic jam achieves nothing except an increase in annoyance for those around you.

Road rage – the Royal Aspect

Most members of the Royal Family avoid the road-rage issue by employing a chauffeur. If a chauffeur is collecting a passenger or group of passengers, he should get out of the car and open the door for them. For a wedding, this duty includes helping the bride or bridesmaids with their skirts and trains, to ensure that these don't get caught in the door. A driver who is taking his employer to collect other guests should remain behind the wheel of the car while the host gets out to greet his guests and open doors for them. If anyone has to sit beside the driver, it should be the host of the party. In exceptional cases, such as when the Duke of Cambridge dispensed with a chauffeur and drove his wife and newborn son home from hospital himself, the front passenger seat is occupied by a security guard. It is entirely up to you whether or not you feel it necessary to follow this example.

It is also up to you whether or not you enter into conversation with a chauffeur, although the well-trained driver will not take the initiative himself.

Her Ladyship realises that employing a chauffeur is beyond the means of many of her readers, but does recommend occasionally indulging in a taxi. This ceases to be an extravagance and becomes a sensible investment any time that traffic congestion, parking or whose turn it is to drive home is likely to become a bone of contention.

- Don't drive in the middle lane of the motorway unless there is a steady stream of slower vehicles in the inside lane. Never drive for any length of time in the outside lane – however fast you are driving, there is bound to be a BMW that wants to overtake.

- Don't park across someone's driveway or in front of a gate that claims to be in constant use. In a car park or street where parking places aren't marked, park close enough to the next car to allow as many vehicles into the space as possible, but not so close that anyone will have trouble opening their door or driving away. You don't want to be dragged out of a meeting or a party to move your car; nor to do you want to come back to find its brake light bashed in by someone trying to edge past.

Getting out of a car

The more low-slung and sporty the car, the more difficult it is for a woman to make an elegant exit. If you know you are going to be in such a car it's a sensible precaution not to wear a short or tight skirt, but whatever you are wearing these tips should help you to keep your dignity intact and your undergarments to yourself.

- Before opening the door, straighten your skirt and pull it down as far as possible.

- Open the door as far as you can without leaning out of the car to push it (if your companion or chauffeur can do this for you, so much the better).

- Keeping your knees firmly together, swivel round on the seat and put both feet on the ground.

- Inch your hips closer to the edge of the seat.

- Before you attempt to stand up, check how high the door is and duck your head if necessary. Then put your hands on the seat on either side of you and push yourself up in one smooth movement. On a windy day, you may prefer to push with one hand and hold your skirt in place with the other.

- Make sure your feet are steady on the ground (car parks are notoriously uneven and pothole-ridden) before taking a step. It would be a shame to let all that effort go to waste by falling flat on your face.

Getting out of a carriage – the Royal Aspect

Surprising though it may sound, this is easier than getting out of a sports car, partly because you are sitting in a more natural and comfortable position in the first place and partly because you are likely to have a footman to help you. When the carriage stops, the footman will open the door and let down the steps. It is customary for a man to descend – unaided – first, and then, if necessary, to give his arm to a woman. She should simply stand up, make sure there is no danger of her skirt's being caught in the steps, and descend slowly and gracefully. It is perfectly acceptable to hold on to the door just as one would hold on to the handrail of a more conventional staircase. A quiet word of thanks to the footman is *de rigueur*.

Cycling

Her Ladyship has to declare a prejudice here – as a pedestrian, she finds the majority of London cyclists an utter nuisance. Cyclists, in her view, should adhere to a number of basic rules that too many of them ignore:

- Ride on the road, not the pavement.
- Obey traffic lights. In particular, acknowledge the fact that red means stop.
- Wear something bright in poor light, and make sure the bicycle's lights are functioning.
- Give clear hand signals in plenty of time before you turn.
- Don't cycle more than two abreast, even on country lanes: cars may appear out of nowhere. Stick to single file in built-up areas.

If she were the mother of a cyclist, she would further add:

- Wear a helmet. You don't want to get yourself killed.

To give token support to the other side of the argument, she also advises motorists to treat cyclists on the road with respect. Give them space, especially when you are overtaking them, and keep out of cycle lanes. One of the reasons cyclists trespass onto pavements is that they feel threatened by motor vehicles: don't let your inconsiderate driving justify this misbehaviour.

Gym etiquette

So many people frequent gyms nowadays that Her Ladyship feels a few pointers are essential. She apologises to her more sensitive readers for the emphasis on underclothing and perspiration:

- Wear appropriate clothing. Various parts of both male and female anatomy require support; outer garments should neither flaunt athletic figures nor give unsympathetic exposure to flabby ones. You are there to improve your fitness, not distract others by an unnecessary display of flesh.

> *Outer garments should neither flaunt athletic figures nor give unsympathetic exposure to flabby ones.*

- Don't take possession of any one piece of equipment. Unless you are exercising in your own private gym, others may be waiting – patiently or otherwise – to use it.

- Wipe equipment down with a towel after you've used it. Then either take the towel home (if it belongs to you) or deposit it in a bin provided in the changing rooms. Don't leave it lying about.

- The same applies to water bottles, apple cores and discarded clothing. Leave the areas in which you have been working out, showering or changing as you would wish to find them and don't expect others to clear up your detritus.

- If you're listening to music (or anything else) through headphones, keep the volume down. As on public transport, don't inflict the tinny drone or the pounding bass of your chosen accompaniment on other people.

- Try not to grunt, however strenuously you are bending or lifting. As anyone who has watched women's tennis over the last twenty years knows, it is not an attractive sound.

- In a swimming pool, follow the prescribed lane etiquette. You are not obliged to plough relentlessly up and down until you have completed ten more lengths than you managed last week, but others will want to – keep out of their way.

- Beware of becoming a gym bore. However excited you are about your own progress, Her Ladyship can assure you that *very* few people care how many reps you have achieved.

4

WHAT TO WEAR WHEN

It would be a stupid person indeed who judged a new acquaintance
merely because he or she was not fashionably…dressed, but it is
natural to feel repulsion for those who wear dirty, torn, ugly,
or vulgar garments. LADY TROUBRIDGE, *THE BOOK OF ETIQUETTE* (1926)

At the time of Her Majesty's Diamond Jubilee there was even
more public interest than usual in the Royal wardrobe and many
common-sense tips were made public: Her Majesty, for example,
favours three-quarter-length, close-fitting sleeves to avoid the risk
of them slopping in soup or being caught on a passing rose bush.

Her dressers also take into consideration the setting in which
Her Majesty is likely to be photographed – she doesn't wear green,
for example, if she is planting a tree in a predominantly green
park. Light fabrics such as chiffon may be discreetly weighted
down so that they don't blow about in a sudden breeze; and on
days when 'quick changes' are required, Her Majesty favours
zipped dresses that she can step in and out of without making
a mess of hair or make-up. These are all considerations that you
can adapt to your own wardrobe.

If, like the Royals, you are likely to be photographed on
more than one special occasion, it is preferable to have more than
one special outfit. Unforgiving paparazzi and people-watching
'journalists' will always notice (and mention) that you are wearing
the same dress and trying to disguise the fact with a pashmina of a
different colour. One British tabloid even recently published (on
its front page) a photograph of the Duchess of Cambridge in a

dress that had been seen a year earlier and made much of her apparent thriftiness – though this same paper would have been the first to criticise Her Royal Highness for extravagance if that had suited their mood of the day. Her Ladyship's guiding rule here has to be 'You can't win', but she also feels strongly that if you have dressed appropriately both to the occasion and to your own age, colouring and figure you cannot have gone far wrong.

With a handful of exceptions, such as Royal Garden Parties and Royal Ascot, dress codes are more relaxed than they used to be. But there are a few occasions when it is necessary – and many more when it can be fun – to dress up. On formal invitations the required dress is usually specified, but it helps to know what the different 'codes' mean.

Dress for men

There isn't space in a book of this size to go into the minutiae of the different styles of jackets, trousers and waistcoats: the following are outlines only. If you are buying or hiring an outfit, a good tailor will advise you on the amount of braid required on the trousers, this year's attitude to silk as opposed to satin lapels and the level of polish required on shoes.

If you need formal wear for a special occasion that is not likely to be repeated, it makes sense to hire. Otherwise, bear in mind that classic tailoring does not quickly go out of fashion and buy the best you can afford. A female friend of Her Ladyship whose wardrobe was limited was invited to Glyndebourne for the

Bear in mind that classic tailoring does not quickly go out of fashion and buy the best you can afford.

second year running and asked nervously if it would matter if she wore the same dress. 'I'll be wearing the same suit,' was her

Decorations – the Royal Aspect

Invitations to state banquets or other particularly grand occasions may include the word 'decorations'. This means that if you are entitled to wear the emblem of a chivalric order such as the Garter, Thistle or Bath, or a military or civilian honour such as the George or Victoria Cross, you are welcome to do so. (It is wrong to wear them if the invitation does not specify them.)

Many members of the Royal Family are entitled to wear these honours. Her Majesty the Queen, for example, is an ex officio member of the Order of the Garter, as is the Prince of Wales. Their Royal Highnesses the Duke of Edinburgh, the Duke of Kent, the Prince Royal, the Duke of Gloucester, Princess Alexandra, The Honourable Lady Ogilvy, the Duke of York, the Earl of Wessex and the Duke of Cambridge are all Royal Knights of the Garter. The Prince of Wales, the Duke of Edinburgh, the Princess Royal and the Duke of Cambridge are also members of the Order of the Thistle and would wear the relevant decorations on state occasions. (The lavish vestments of the various Orders, including the long velvet mantle and velvet hat adorned with feathers, are reserved for ceremonial occasions of the Orders themselves.)

Most orders – whether worn by Royals or non-Royals – are suspended from a metal bar on the left breast of a jacket or dress, although it is permissible to wear one on a ribbon round the neck; the ribbon should be tucked under the shirt collar and its length carefully calculated so that the decoration hangs just below the bow tie.

If the decoration includes a sash, this should be worn on white-tie occasions, but not with less formal attire. Decorations are often worn, for example, with dark suits or overcoats on Remembrance Sunday, when sashes would be entirely inappropriate.

On state occasions when decorations are on display, women may wear tiaras, which should always be family heirlooms. No one with any claims to good breeding would ever buy a tiara. Her Ladyship advises, however, that a tiara always give the wearer a rather *grande dame* look. For a long time tiaras were considered the prerogative of the married woman; nowadays Her Ladyship would be inclined to specify a married woman of a certain age. On the young tiaras look flashy and – passing quickly over Her Ladyship's recent remark about good breeding – are best chosen for their cheapness and reserved for hen parties.

escort's comforting reply. A good-quality suit worn two or three times a year will earn its keep – and its share of compliments – much more readily than a job lot of half a dozen for the same price.

Black tie is the most commonly worn style of formal dress, appropriate for evening parties and weddings; it is not often worn during the day except to country-house opera such as Glyndebourne. It consists of a black suit rather than the tailcoat required for morning dress, but with silk lapels and a bow tie to match them; a white dress shirt with a pleated front; black cummerbund or low-cut waistcoat; black bow tie; black socks and shoes.

Morning dress is worn only at Royal Ascot, formal weddings and the like; it consists of a black or grey tailcoat with striped trousers; a top hat the same colour as the coat; waistcoat and tie of no specific colour, but not too garish; black socks and shoes.

White tie: the most formal of all, unlikely to be needed unless you are invited to a state banquet. It comprises a black evening tailcoat (subtly different in style from a morning coat); black rather than striped trousers; black top hat (not worn during the banquet itself, of course); white stiff-fronted shirt with detachable collar; white waistcoat; white bow tie; black socks and shoes. If you need a watch it should be of the kind you can carry in a pocket – it is considered bad form to wear a wrist watch with 'white tie'. Bear in mind also that a dress shirt has no buttons at the cuffs and therefore requires a set of cuff links.

Black is the only acceptable colour for shoes to accompany any formal attire. Brown shoes, the purists say, should be worn only with tweeds, and tweeds should be worn only in the country.

For less formal occasions, 'smart casual' doesn't require a suit, but it does suggest a blazer or sports jacket and a tie. Even if you are told to 'come as you are', at the very least you should change out of the clothes you have been wearing to mow the lawn, then shower, shave and make sure your fingernails are scrupulously clean. But the sartorial rules are very relaxed, permitting shorts and tee-shirt for a summer barbecue, or jeans and sweater for a kitchen supper party. Shoes can be comfortable but must be clean.

Dress for women

The degree of formality of dress is generally indicated by the length of the skirt, with the most formal occasions demanding a floor-length gown. Traditionally this is permitted to expose the shoulders and a good deal of bosom, but discretion is advisable if there is to be

An energetic Highland reel can play havoc with a low-cut dress and its contents.

dancing. An energetic Highland reel (still frequently part of the programme at elegant Scottish parties) can play havoc with a low-cut dress and its contents.

A long dress that doesn't quite justify the appellation 'gown' is appropriate for an evening 'black tie' occasion, but would run the risk of looking overdressed during the day or for an early evening drinks party. For these, a long skirt with a silk blouse or a formal day dress, with a skirt at or below the knee, would be a better choice; an elegant trouser suit might also be acceptable. 'Smart casual' means you should leave the tiara and Ascot hat at home, but still allows you to wear a pretty dress with a jacket or tailored trousers with a crisp blouse. The 'come as you are' rules are similar to those for men (see above) – the most casual invitation still requires cleanliness and the suggestion of an iron. If in doubt, check with your host.

Shoes

A note when choosing which shoes to wear: remember that you are going to be wearing them for some hours and possibly standing or dancing for much of that time. Your feet are – Her Ladyship can find no more elegant way of phrasing this – likely to swell up and become hot and sticky. Removing your shoes in the middle of a formal party is not only bad form, it will make people think you have over-imbibed. As a precaution, particularly with new shoes, 'break them in' by wearing them with socks for a few hours at home first. This will both stretch them a little and simulate the effect of slightly larger-than-usual feet.

Avoid stilettos if you are likely to be standing or walking on a lawn, whether at a Royal Garden Party or at a friend's barbecue. Stilettos are, of course, *non grata* on a bowling green or polo pitch.

Overdressed versus underdressed

One fashion precept maintains that it is better to be overdressed than underdressed: dressing smartly shows that you have paid your host the compliment of making an effort, and it is easier to remove gloves and jewellery (or a jacket and tie) to make an outfit less formal than it is to 'dress up' jeans and a sweater.

On the other hand, overdressing can make other people feel uncomfortable – as if they have failed to make the effort. Elegant is always better than flashy except at a fancy-dress party or hen night, and the 'less is more' maxim is never more true than with jewellery – think Grace Kelly or Catherine Zeta-Jones.

Dress sense – the Royal Aspect

The question of how flattering or otherwise your outfit is – too rarely asked by young women on their way to Royal Ascot of recent years – is of overwhelming importance if anyone is likely to be following you with a camera. The more high-profile you are, the more interest others will take in your every move and the more readers of tabloid newspapers and celebrity-obsessed magazines will lap up any fashion flaws. They will also have strong (if utterly impertinent) views on whether you are too fat or too thin.

Now that everyone carries a telephone with an inbuilt camera, even those who are of no interest to the paparazzi run the risk of being made to look ridiculous. A bulging midriff, eye-catching décolleté and stagger-inducing heels may not make it to the tabloids, but there is every chance they will be splashed over someone's Facebook page before the night is out.

Her Ladyship's advice? Look in the mirror, at your back view as well as your front, before you leave home.

Special occasions

Many of the traditional events of the London 'Season' have become more casual over the years; one or two of them, in an understandable backlash against the dropping of standards, have become more rigid. Royal Ascot recently revised its dress code for the Royal Enclosure and insists on 'skirts of a modest length', with just above the knee being the shortest admissible. Strapless tops are not permitted; nor are skimpy straps or bare midriffs, although smart trouser suits are. Hats or substantial headpieces with a base of at least 4in (10cm) must be worn. Her Ladyship wholeheartedly agrees with the Royal Ascot organisers, who believe that 'a day out at Ascot Racecourse is very special and dressing for the occasion is an important part of the raceday experience' (though she cannot help deploring their lack of hyphen in race-day).

The Stewards' Enclosure at Henley Royal Regatta is not quite so formal, but is every bit as strict in enforcing its rules. Ladies must not wear short skirts, divided skirts, culottes or trousers of any kind. For men, a lounge suit or jacket or blazer with flannels, and a tie or cravat are required. Royal Ascot employs what the disrespectful call 'the fashion police' to hand out ties or pashminas to those who have come unsuitably dressed; at Henley you are likely simply to be refused admission.

If you are fortunate enough to be invited to a Royal Garden Party, your invitation will include instructions on what to wear. A smart day dress and hat is the norm for women; men wear morning dress or lounge suits.

Whatever the occasion and whatever your gender, Service Dress is considered correct attire for a member of the armed forces. Visitors from overseas will also be welcome in the formal national dress of their country.

Wedding dress

Female guests should feel free to be colourful,
particularly at spring and summer weddings. The one
taboo is a predominantly white outfit, white being the
bride's prerogative. Black is also considered somewhat
pessimistic; if your only possible choice is a little black
dress, enliven it with accessories in bright pink, yellow
or some other cheerful colour.

5

FORMAL DINNERS

Table manners are no longer about adhering to a rigid, and outdated, code of conduct. They exist for guidance but shouldn't take away from the pleasure of sharing a meal.

JO BRYANT, ETIQUETTE ADVISOR FOR DEBRETT'S, 2012

The form and formality of any invitation should be appropriate to the occasion. If you plan to entertain a Royal, the date must be arranged (via the Royal personage's private secretary) and your proposed guest list approved before anyone else is invited. Invitations to your other guests are then phrased as offering 'the honour of meeting Her Royal Highness Princess X'.

At the other end of the formality scale, by all means email or text close friends to ask if they want to come for supper on Saturday. For something bigger such as an informal birthday celebration, housewarming or Hallowe'en party, you may want to send written or printed invitations through the post or as an attachment to an email. The design facilities that modern computers put at your disposal can produce something quirky, personal and entirely appropriate. However, this DIY approach is less suited to formal occasions such as a wedding or a dinner given by a livery company, embassy or regiment.

The best quality invitations are still engraved on card and good stationers can advise on this. Good stationers are, sadly, a dying breed, but Her Ladyship knows of one in London that supplied members of Queen Victoria's family and celebrities such as Lily Langtry and maintains the high standards that many people look for on special occasions. Alternatively and more cheaply, printed cards may be ordered from one of the many websites offering this service. Try to use one that has been recommended by someone whose taste you trust. Be careful, too, over your choice of design and for wedding invitations you should certainly

Good stationers are, sadly, a dying breed, but Her Ladyship knows of one in London that supplied members of Queen Victoria's family...

err on the side of simplicity and elegance. It is not for nothing that graphic designers spend time studying the rules of typography: there are few things less attractive than badly arranged type in a mishmash of styles.

The cards should come with envelopes that are exactly the right size, of a suitable quality and have pointed flaps. Straight flaps are appropriate for business correspondence, but unattractive with invitations or personal correspondence.

Make sure you see a proof to check before it is too late to make corrections. When checking, remember the proof-reader's maxim: the larger the type, the easier it is to overlook a mistake. Her Ladyship was once asked to glance over a draft of a friend's change of address card and noticed that although the printers had been meticulous as to new phone number and postcode, they had misspelled the friend's surname – an error that the friend whose name it was had failed to spot.

What should an invitation say?

Any invitation, however formal or informal, must tell the recipient what to expect. If there is a dress code, it should say so (see Chapter 4 (page 60–65) for more details of what the various 'codes' mean). It should also make clear where the party is taking place (particularly important if you are holding a party other than in your own home), when it starts and finishes and what form of refreshment is being provided. 'Cocktails and canapés 6–8pm' warns guests that they must expect to dine (at their own expense) afterwards; 'buffet supper' suggests they should emerge well fed. By all means put 'eight till late' on an invitation to a party in your own home if you aren't bothered what time you get to bed; 'carriages at 11.30pm' or, as a friend of Her Ladyship with a theatrical bent put it, '11.30pm: *exeunt omnes*' is useful for older party-givers who *do* care what time they go to bed or if the party is in a hired venue that has to be vacated at a given time. If there is to be dancing, the invitation should mention this, too, to enable guests to make an appropriate choice of clothes and shoes.

Accepting and refusing

Invitations from Her Majesty and from other senior members of the Royal Family are generally considered commands: it isn't done to plead a prior commitment. In most other circumstances, you may send your regrets if you are otherwise engaged. The more important the occasion, though, the more substantial your reason for declining should be. A friend of Her Ladyship was once understandably put out because another friend turned down an invitation to her wedding. This was admittedly a small-scale affair arranged at comparatively short notice and the friend in question had just moved house. Even so, the bride felt that needing to wait in for the plumber was an unflattering excuse for being absent from such a special event.

As for accepting invitations, there two simple rules: once you have accepted, you turn up, and you don't turn up without accepting. Influential newspaper columnists and reviewers who could attend three launch parties every night of their lives if they so wished have been known to arrive without telling anyone that they are going to do so, confident that their appearance will be greeted with delight by the publicist doing the organising. The fact that they are probably right doesn't alter Her Ladyship's opinion that it is an arrogant thing to do; if everybody did it, it would play complete havoc with the catering arrangements, not to mention the host's nerves.

That said, *force majeure* may enter into all our lives at unforeseen moments and make cancelling an engagement inevitable. Cancellations should always be accompanied by sincere (or sincere-sounding) apologies and valid (or valid-sounding) excuses. They should also be made as soon as possible. The rules about cancelling a hotel reservation are a useful analogy here: the financial penalties are negligible if you do it a month in advance; if you cancel on the day or simply don't put in an appearance, you pay the full price. The parallels between being able to re-let the hotel room and being able to invite another guest at short notice are obvious.

So too are the parallels between the levels of annoyance and inconvenience caused. You cannot be expected to predict that you are going to wake up with a migraine on the day of a party, or that one of your family is going to be involved in an accident; in those circumstances of course you have to pull out at the last minute. But if you acquire the reputation for being an unreliable guest, cancelling for no good reason (and leading your host to suspect that you have had a better offer), you will soon find the invitations drying up. You should no more be cavalier about having supper with a neighbour than you should about going to receive an OBE from the monarch – not least because the

You should no more be cavalier about having supper with a neighbour than you should about going to receive an OBE from the monarch.

neighbour, unlike the monarch, probably does her own shopping and will have gone to some trouble on your behalf.

And, while she is at this less formal end of the scale, Her Ladyship has to express annoyance at those people who seem incapable of committing to a date. If, for example, two friends plan to go to the cinema together and Friend A says, 'I could do these three dates', it is incumbent on Friend B to respond promptly. As with unpunctuality, where it is rude to behave as if your time is more important than anyone else's, so it is bad manners to assume that a friend's social life is so impoverished that he or she can keep three evenings free indefinitely, pending your convenience.

Eating habits

Invitations to formal dinners will often give you the opportunity to express a dietary requirement when you send your acceptance, so

that you can advise the host or organiser that you eat kosher, are vegetarian or have to avoid gluten. If they don't, telephone well in advance and explain your needs.

Her Ladyship uses the word 'needs' advisedly here: while cultural or health considerations are valid, fads are not. If you have an aversion to cabbage and cabbage is served at the meal, either refuse it politely if it is being served to you, or move it unobtrusively to the side of your plate if you are presented with a *fait accompli*. Refusing it politely means saying, 'No, thank you' in an impassive tone and leaving it at that. A busy waiter would prefer not to be told that cabbage will make you sick or have any other unpleasant physical effect.

There is no need to make a fuss, either, about not drinking alcohol. Just ask for something soft. A waiter will not query this; friends may be less discreet. 'I'm driving' should be an unanswerable explanation; 'It's January' will be acceptable in many circles (providing that it is indeed January). If you have given up for reasons you prefer not to discuss, have an excuse ready. 'I'm on antibiotics' is better than 'I'm trying to cut down' or 'I'm trying to lose weight', both of which may provoke the unthinking response, 'One glass won't hurt you.' If you do normally imbibe, you must expect to be teased if you give up, but stick to your guns – and if there is a serious reason for your abstemiousness, tell close friends quietly later.

Seating plans

At a large formal meal with many tables, there may be a chart near the entrance indicating where everyone is to sit. The tables will be numbered, with the top table – number one – at the front or in the centre of the room. Check where you are meant to be so that, when everyone is invited to take their seats, you can do so quickly and without fuss. At the table, your place will be marked by a card bearing your name.

A single large table will also have name cards to indicate where everyone should sit. Except when there is an honoured guest who must be placed next to the host (see the box opposite), men and women are usually seated alternately, and partners are separated. Traditionally, a man should pull out the chair of the woman to his right and ensure she is comfortable before sitting down himself.

You were once expected to talk only to your immediate neighbours; it was considered pert to converse with someone sitting across the table from you, although this may have been because the size of the table meant you had to shout or because there were enormous centrepieces that were difficult to see round. Nowadays the rule is less rigidly enforced, though shouting is still considered rude.

Even if the first course is already on the table when you sit down, don't pick up a knife, fork, spoon or glass until your host does. A toast or, in some settings, a prayer may be said and it is disrespectful to start tucking in before these formalities are out of the way.

Place settings

Those unaccustomed to formal place settings are often intimidated by the array of cutlery and glasses in front of them. But the rule for cutlery is simple: start at the outside and work inwards towards the plate. If the first course is soup, you should find a round-bowled spoon to the far right of your plate. Otherwise there will probably be a small knife to the right and a small fork to the left. Inside this, closer to

The rule for cutlery is simple: start at the outside and work inwards towards the plate.

the plate, will be a larger knife and fork for the main course, a spoon and perhaps a fork for the pudding, and so on. Your napkin may be intricately arranged in the centre, in the place where your plate will go, or neatly folded on your bread plate, which is always to your left. The knife on this plate is for butter and should not be used for the bread itself: correct form is to place a portion of butter on the side of your plate, tear a small piece off the roll, butter it and eat it before tearing off the next piece.

The arrangement of glasses is slightly more complicated than that of cutlery, because it depends on the number and nature of wines being served. It is, however, largely based on common sense, with the smaller glasses closer to you. Thus you may find four glasses arranged in a square: bottom left, closest to you, is the white wine glass, with the larger glass for red wine behind it. Bottom right, next to the white wine glass, is one for water and behind it, if required, a champagne flute.

Seating arrangements – the Royal Aspect

At most official dinners, the host is seated at the centre of the table, with the most important guest on his right. Other guests are then seated in order of precedence, the highest ranking being nearest to the host. The exception is if the guest is Her Majesty the Queen, in which case she takes the host's place at the centre of things, while he sits to her right. Other Royal guests take precedence over non-Royals.

At formal dinners, there will be a waiter to refill your glass. Never lift it towards him – that smacks of desperation. A trained waiter can reach between you and your neighbour to pour without disturbing anyone or spilling wine on the table. If you don't want any more, put your hand lightly over the top of your glass and say, 'No, thank you' (or 'Not at the moment, thank you' if you want to pace yourself but keep your options open for later). White wine is frequently served with the first course and red with the main; if red wine gives you a migraine say quietly to the waiter, 'Could I possibly stick to white?' If, however, it is white wine to which you object, you will have to be patient: it is rude to upset the waiters' routine by demanding red wine ahead of schedule. In a similar vein, don't demand a whisky and soda or a beer during the course of the meal. If you must drink these drinks, acquire one in the bar beforehand and bring it to the table with you.

Using cutlery

Move a soup spoon away from you in order to gather up the soup, then drink from the side of the spoon, not the tip. As your bowl empties, tip it away from you in order to pick up the last spoonfuls.

When using a knife and fork together, keep the tines of the fork face downwards. Only the fork goes in your mouth. In elegant company, it is not done to put down your knife, transfer your fork to your other hand and use it as a spoon to eat, for example, peas or rice. Use your knife to press these into the back of the fork.

With pudding, raise only the spoon to your mouth. A pudding fork is supplied to help you hold something like pastry in position while you cut it with the edge of your spoon; it may also help you to gather up errant mouthfuls.

If your food is accompanied by a lemon wedge, pick it up in one hand and press or twist your fork into it. This results in a more controlled flow of juice and means you are less likely to squirt your neighbour in the eye than if you squeeze the lemon with your fingers.

When you put your cutlery down on your plate between mouthfuls, use a criss-cross pattern (or leave a lone spoon at an angle). This will show a passing waiter that you haven't finished. When you *have* finished, line the cutlery up neatly with the handles facing you.

Basic table manners

Her Ladyship hopes her readers were taught these things as toddlers, so she will give only the briefest of recaps:

• Keep your elbows to yourself. It is perfectly possible to cut even a steak or handle a corn cob without jabbing your neighbour.

• Don't slurp, gobble or eat with your mouth open. Take small mouthfuls and put your cutlery down on your plate between each one to allow yourself time to chew and swallow before filling your mouth again.

• Don't, under any circumstances, talk with your mouth full. That *bon mot* will just have to go unuttered if the conversational moment for it passes before you have finished chewing.

• If you find something in your mouth that you can't easily swallow – a fish bone or piece of shot from a game bird, for example – cup your hand over your mouth, spit the offending article out as unobtrusively as possible and put it on the side of your plate.

- Don't tuck your napkin into your clothing – spread it out on your lap and use it to dab the corners of your mouth when you have finished eating. Her Ladyship has noticed that David Suchet's Poirot disobeys the first part of this rule, but puts that down to his obsessive concern with not dirtying his clothes; she cannot deny that he dabs his mouth with great delicacy.

- If you choke or find yourself with hiccups, ask for a glass of water if one is not to hand. Excuse yourself from the table rather than cough and splutter all over your fellow guests.

- If you need to excuse yourself for other, more personal reasons, try to wait until an interval between courses. A thoughtful host will seat the elderly or the heavily pregnant near the door so that this sort of exit can be made discreetly – if, as a guest, you think this is going to be necessary, try to warn your host in advance.

Don't just help yourself

Good table manners involve making sure other people have what they need. If you have bread, butter, salt, pepper or anything else that is to be shared with others within easy reach, offer it to your neighbour before helping yourself. If not, never stretch across someone else – ask them if they would pass it and, once it is in your possession, offer it to others first. If someone asks you for the salt but not the pepper, or vice versa, pass both, so that the two remain together.

Conversation

The easiest way to start a conversation with a stranger is to ask him about himself. 'How do you know [our host]?' is the most obvious

A note on smoking

Never excuse yourself during a formal meal to 'nip out' for a cigarette, however desperate you may feel. Before smoking was banned in public places in the UK, smokers at formal dinners had to wait until after the Loyal Toast (to the reigning monarch) was given before they were permitted to indulge; nowadays the same rule applies, except that smokers go to a designated smoking area rather than lighting up at the table. On one lavish occasion shortly after the ban came into force in England in 2007, The Worshipful Company of Tobacco Pipe Makers and Tobacco Blenders apparently circumvented the need to send smokers outside by providing each of their guests with a helping of snuff, but they presumably had a plentiful supply to hand and could expect their guests to take a professional interest. In other companies this may not be to everyone's taste.

gambit; Her Ladyship has one acquaintance who prefers 'Tell me about you'. She also had a lively elderly relative who once sat down at a charity dinner and asked the man sitting next to her, to whom she had only just been introduced, 'So what are we going to talk about?' It has to be said that this approach threw her companion for a moment, but he recovered and they spent a stimulating hour agreeing wholeheartedly on the importance of teaching Latin in schools.

The point of asking someone about themselves is not to be vulgarly inquisitive but to find common ground: the request 'Tell me about you' might elicit the answer that the person concerned had just returned from a business trip to Malawi, or was passionate about gardening, Italian cinema or classic cars. It is then up to you to say something more encouraging than 'How interesting.' Perhaps you have always wanted to go to Malawi – or have never given the place a thought, in which case you can ask what took your companion there, what his impressions were and whether he would recommend it for a holiday. Perhaps your interests lie in cookery, Hollywood westerns and horse-riding, so you can put a case for your own preferences and spark a gentle debate. Remember, however, to give your companion time to express his or her views before jumping in with yours, and be careful to listen to what they are saying rather than preparing what you are going to say the moment they give you the opportunity. Conversation is not meant to be a monologue, nor is it a Q & A session: it's a mutual exploring of ideas and enthusiasms.

A friend of Her Ladyship recently had a tedious experience at a dinner party when the man she was sitting next to had obviously not absorbed the rules of conversational dialogue. Before the first course was over, she knew that he was a solicitor in a high-flying City firm and what his annual bonus was likely to be for the next five years; that he had studied law at Durham, having failed to get into Oxford because of the extraordinary modern prejudice against applicants from public schools; that his father had fought in the Falklands War; and that the reasons why the country was going to the dogs were many and various. 'All very fascinating,' remarked Her Ladyship's friend dryly, 'but I don't think he even asked my name, never mind anything about me.'

Certain subjects remain taboo, however. Discussing money – how much you are paid, how much others in your profession are paid, what you paid for your house, car, children's education or new dress – is unarguably vulgar. Politics, religion and sex are all to be avoided unless you have some idea of the opinions of everyone within earshot. While arguing among friends on these subjects can be both thought-provoking and enjoyable, you can cause great offence by pontificating about the shortcomings of the Prime Minister, the ordination of women or your views on the Common Agricultural Policy if what you assume is an

You have no way of knowing whether the person to whom you have just been introduced is discreet or … 'as leaky as a chocolate teapot'.

open-and-shut case doesn't accord with the opinions of the stranger sitting next to you. Your own health and personal problems are also unlikely to be of interest to a new acquaintance.

Remember, too, that you have no way of knowing whether the person to whom you have just been introduced is discreet or, as a gossipy friend of Her Ladyship was once described, 'as leaky as a chocolate teapot'. If you don't want what you say getting back to your host or a mutual friend, or appearing on the front page of next Sunday's papers, be very careful what you confide in someone you don't know well.

6

EATING OUT

Serenely full, the Epicure would say,
Fate cannot harm me, I have dined to-day.

THE REVEREND SYDNEY SMITH, *RECIPE FOR SALAD* (1839)

It is not usual to entertain Royalty in a restaurant: the security implications and the risk of attracting unwanted attention are too great. When the Duke and Duchess of Cambridge chose to take lunch in a historic pub rather than a Michelin-starred restaurant, the arrangement was made a month in advance and the pub closed to other customers.

Even when security and the paparazzi are not a worry, eating in restaurants can cause anxiety. For women, until about the 1950s, it was a comparatively straightforward matter: you were taken by a man – your father, brother, boyfriend (once he had been approved by your parents) or, in due course, husband. He made the arrangements and paid the bill. Some country gentlewomen or sophisticated businesswomen might belong to a London club where she could entertain, but even then the demarcation between host and guest was clear. As with so many other areas of etiquette, however, modern waters are rather muddier.

Where shall we go?

Choosing which restaurant to go to has traditionally been the responsibility of the host; if you are the one issuing the invitation and expecting to pay the bill, this is still the case today. However, even a simple-sounding guideline such as this can be fraught with difficulty and Her Ladyship would once again emphasise the maxim, 'Think about the other person.' A colleague of hers once arranged to take an important potential client to a stylish (and expensive) Indian restaurant, hoping to impress him. Unfortunately he failed to ask the client if he liked Indian food. The meal was rendered awkward by the client's peering suspiciously at every dish he was offered, ostentatiously pushing unfamiliar vegetables to the side of his plate and constantly asking for more water. Her Ladyship refrains from commenting on the client's manners; her point is that subsequent business relations did not prosper.

When a group of friends meet casually to 'go out for a meal', choice of location should be mutual and should take into consideration the tastes and budgets of all concerned. Her Ladyship has two friends who are frequently at mild loggerheads over this: one is always eager to try the latest fashionable eatery and is prepared to pay the price; the other is both less adventurous and less prosperous and would be happy in the local pizzeria. The result, to paraphrase the Lerner and Loewe song from *My Fair Lady*, is that all too often 'rather than do either they go somewhere else that neither likes at all'. Her Ladyship is of the opinion that a little more flexibility on both sides would be beneficial: the richer one should perhaps reserve her extravagances

The result is that all too often 'rather than do either they go somewhere else that neither likes at all'.

for special occasions, while the other could make an effort to please her friend by being a little less conservative. There is one unarguable point to be made here, though: it is rude to inveigle someone into spending more money (on a meal or any other form of entertainment) than they are comfortable with or, even worse, to force them to admit that they can't afford it.

In the restaurant

It is considered good manners for the host (or the man in a mixed couple) to sit with his back to the room; the guest or the woman should have the 'view'.

Now that dining out casually with friends is a common occurrence, many people pay their own way much of the time. This is not true on a business occasion, when the person who has arranged the meeting should still expect to pay. If you invite friends to a restaurant and want to pay – to thank them for a kindness or because you can't cook and don't want to embarrass yourself by inviting them for supper – make it clear from the outset that this is your treat. Then make sure you go to a restaurant you can afford: it takes some of the generosity out of your gesture if you

Make sure you go to a restaurant you can afford: it takes some of the generosity out of your gesture if you pointedly guide your guests towards a set menu.

pointedly guide your guests towards a set menu when they might prefer to choose from the à la carte. No one with any claim to manners will order foie gras followed by lobster at someone else's expense, but the sensible host should be prepared for them to do so – or take them to a restaurant where they will not be exposed to this expensive temptation.

Even if it has been made clear that one person is intending to pay, well-mannered guests will offer to contribute their share; the host should refuse the offer firmly but graciously, and the guests should then back down without further ado. If it seems appropriate they may pay for a further round of drinks or the taxi home; otherwise they should accept the generosity in the spirit in which it is intended and say, 'On me next time.' One way to avoid any dispute over the bill is for the host to go to the loo when the meal is almost over; he or she can then discreetly stop at the bar or the till and pay before returning to the table.

The guest who will barely eat at all is, in his or her own way, every bit as troublesome as the one who orders foie gras and lobster. If your diet is restricted for cultural or health reasons, warn your host in advance. Once in the restaurant, don't make a commotion about your need for dairy-free or whatever it may be: choose something that looks as if it will suit your requirements, ask the waiter (quietly) to confirm that it does and have an alternative choice ready in case it doesn't. Many restaurants will omit an offending sauce if requested to do so. Don't confuse a dislike of a certain food with an allergy: if your plate appears with something unheralded that you don't like, push it quietly to one side and eat round it. Only if you are genuinely likely to be physically unwell or suffer from anaphylactic shock should you ask for the plate to be taken away altogether.

If your difficulty is that you have a very small appetite, there is no disgrace in ordering two starters, even if the first one is a tiny salad. But no one should be forced into eating more than they want to, so if you want only one course, say so and make it clear that you are happy to sip wine or water while everyone else has a first course. Do *not* use your abstemiousness to make anyone else feel greedy. Her Ladyship once went to a restaurant with an acquaintance who rebuked her for the amount of wine she drank with dinner, conveniently forgetting that she had herself had three large whiskies beforehand. Some fifteen years later, Her Ladyship still allows that to rankle.

Ordering

Purists maintain that the host should do the ordering for everyone at the table, so you should convey your wishes to him (or her). If necessary, the waiter will then ask you how you like your steak, or tell you that the duck is normally served pink. It is perfectly correct to have that part of the conversation direct with the waiter. If you want to order anything more – for example, if you discover that vegetables are not included – ask your host rather than charging ahead.

If you are all paying your own way, this formality can be dispensed with and everyone will order for themselves. Take your lead from the waiter, though, as to the way you order, especially if you are a large group. He may prefer to take all the orders for first course first; or he may ask each individual for first and second courses together. This makes no difference to you, the customer, but may make it easier for him, so be obliging. Remember, however much fun you are having, he is trying to do his job and serve other customers too, so don't be boisterous or frivolous until the formalities are out of the way.

A note on pre-theatre dining

If you are in a hurry, say so as soon as you arrive. Restaurants near theatres and concert halls often offer a set menu that enables you to be in and out quickly – take advantage of this, or order only one course. It is unreasonable to expect a busy restaurant to allow you to jump the queue just because you haven't allowed yourself sufficient time to eat. Of course, the sensible thing is to book in early and give yourself and your guests plenty of time to enjoy the meal.

Wine in restaurants

It is normally the host who orders the wine, but there is no need to be intimidated about this: wine waiters are, contrary to what many people believe, there to help you. Here are a few basic tips to assist the uninitiated:

- White wine is generally considered the best choice to accompany fish and chicken, while red wine goes better with red meat or game, but the likes and dislikes of your guests should take precedence over these rules. Many people are happy to drink a light red wine with a meaty fish such as tuna, or a hearty white with duck. Some simply prefer one colour to another, no matter what they are eating. Ask your guests what they would like.

- There is no disgrace in ordering the house wine: no self-respecting restaurant will recommend rubbish.

- If you know that one of your guests is more knowledgeable about wine than you are, ask him or her to choose for you. Many people also regard this as a courteous gesture if you are a woman taking a man out, though unless he is particularly well informed about wine he should bow to your choice.

- If you prefer, tell the wine waiter what you have ordered to eat and ask for his advice. To avoid embarrassment if there are expensive wines on the list, point out two or three at a price you are happy to pay and ask him to choose between them.

Once you have made your choice, the wine will be brought to your table and opened in front of you. If it has a cork, the waiter will show this to you, to establish that it is intact and that there is none of the unpleasant aroma that characterises 'corked' wine. He will then pour a small amount for you to try.

There is an element of ritual about this, although you should be careful not to cross the thin line between ritual and palaver. Pick up your glass by the stem and gently swirl the wine around to release its flavours. Sniff it and, if it is not obviously unpleasant, take a sip. Hold the wine in your mouth for a moment before swallowing it. You should then be able to smile at the waiter and say, 'That's fine, thank you'; he will pour it for the rest of the table and fill your glass last. If there is something wrong, now is the moment to say so: some faults, such as the wine's being too warm or too cold, can easily be remedied, but if you really don't like it, you can ask for it to be replaced.

There is an element of ritual about this, although you should be careful not to cross the thin line between ritual and palaver.

Once the wine has been approved, many restaurants will place the bottle on a side table, on the bar or – if it is white or rosé – in an ice bucket a little way away from you. The wine waiter will then keep an eye on the level in everyone's glass and top them up as required. Some waiters are overly assiduous about this, topping up the moment someone has taken a sip. If this is the case, simply say, 'No, thank you' or put your fingers over the top of your glass as he approaches. Or, if the waiter is too intrusive, ask for the wine to be left within reach so that you can pour it yourself. This may not accord with the strict etiquette of the most formal restaurants, but it is one instance in which Her Ladyship feels you are entitled to say (quietly, to yourself), 'I'm the customer' and have it your own way.

That said, Her Ladyship feels obliged to add a warning against taking the 'I'm the customer' attitude too far. A friend of hers once had to do business with a famous gastronome who was also a particularly difficult man. Taking him to a no-more-than-averagely smart restaurant for dinner, she asked him to look at the wine list on her behalf. He courteously obtained her approval of his choice of red, but then said to the (very young) wine waiter, 'Don't bother to decant it.' The poor boy, already awe-struck at the prospect of serving a television personality, obviously had no idea that some red wines should be decanted before serving. The remark had been spitefully calculated to make the waiter feel small.

An extreme example, perhaps, but worth citing as a reminder that waiters – like cleaners and the staff at call centres – are often doing poorly paid jobs for want of anything better and should be treated with consideration. It's also worth noting that this client didn't behave badly to Her Ladyship's friend, who was in a senior position and had influence over how their negotiations would proceed; he turned the malice that he felt towards most of the human race on someone whose views made no difference to him and who wasn't in a position to retaliate. Her Ladyship does not use the word 'unforgivable' lightly, but she felt that this behaviour came close.

Attracting attention

Good waiters keep an eye on their tables and know when
something is needed. If this doesn't happen – or if you
have a request that the waiter hasn't anticipated – raise
your hand slightly (not way above your head, as if you were
a schoolchild asking permission to leave the room) and try
to catch his eye. If you have your back to the room the
movement of swivelling round in your chair often helps. If
necessary call, 'Excuse me.' (Her Ladyship emphasises the
word 'call' rather than 'yell' here.) On no account snap
your fingers and, even in a French restaurant, never
address the waiter as *garçon*. It also means 'boy' and is
offensive and patronising.

Difficult foods

With many awkward-to-eat foods, the answer is to use your fingers,
even in a smart restaurant. If you are uncomfortable about this, it
may be better not to order the food, but Her Ladyship assures her
readers that in most cases it is possible to achieve delicacy and
maintain dignity while dispensing with the convention of a knife
and fork. This list also includes foods that are not difficult to eat
but entail their own etiquette.

If a food with which you are unfamiliar is served at a private
house or at a formal dinner, wait for your host to tackle it and copy
him or her. Or, if need be, ask: there's no shame in admitting that
you have never eaten an artichoke before.

Asparagus: if this is served on its own as a first course, pick each spear up in your fingers and nibble from the tip down to the point where the stem becomes hard. Leave that last bit on your plate. If the asparagus is served with butter or hollandaise sauce in a communal dish, take a little onto your plate and dip each spear into it. It is bad manners to dunk into a dish that other people will also be using.

If asparagus appears in a salad or as an accompaniment to the main course, chop it into bite-sized pieces with a knife and fork as you would any other vegetable.

Cheese: always serve yourself using the cheese knife provided on the cheese board, never with your own butter knife. With a whole round cheese such as a camembert, cut a triangular slice as you would from a cake and use the prongs of the knife to pick it up and deposit it on your plate. With a wedge, cut a slice from the side rather than the pointed end and, again, pick it up with the prongs of the cheese knife. If a cheese slicer (which looks a bit like a pie server with a slit across the middle of the blade) is provided, use this for hard cheeses: pare thin slices from the top of the cheese by pulling the slicer towards you. Some people provide different styles of knife for different styles of cheese: a wedge shape is intended for hard cheese, a thinner blade for soft cheese, with the bell-shaped or campana knife for those in between, known as firm or semi-soft. If only two knives are provided for several types of cheese, reserve one for strong blues such as Stilton and use the other for everything else.

Corn on the cob is so awkward to eat elegantly that it's probably best not to attempt it in public.

Corn on the cob: the exception that proves the rule, this is so difficult to eat elegantly that it's probably best not to attempt it in public unless you are at a barbecue with very close friends. Corn on the cob is often served with small, purpose-designed forks stuck in the ends; if not, it's an invitation to use your fingers. Nibble as delicately as you can, starting at one end and working towards the other, rather than chomping into the middle.

Globe artichokes: these look a bit like overgrown green pine cones and are nothing to do with Jerusalem artichokes, which in their raw state resemble root ginger. Globe artichokes are served whole. Remove the leaves one by one with your fingers and bite off the succulent base. Put the rest of the leaf to one side and pile the leaves up neatly as you progress. As with asparagus, it's easy to tell how much to eat – an artichoke leaf has a nice bit and a nasty bit. Like asparagus, too, artichokes may be served with melted butter or a dipping sauce and the same rule applies: take a portion onto your plate and dip the leaves into that.

At the base of the artichoke is a fleshy 'heart', which is sometimes removed before serving; if it is included, eat it with a knife and fork, being careful to avoid any of the inedible fibrous 'choke' that may have been left in by mistake.

Grapes: not difficult to eat, but the frequent cause of a breach of etiquette. Never, unless you are at home alone with no one to offend, pull individual grapes off a bunch, leaving unsightly stems. Instead, snip a small cluster from the main bunch and don't pull the grapes off the stems until they are on your plate. Elegant hosts will provide special grape scissors for this purpose.

Mussels: holding each shell in one hand, use a fork to loosen the mussel and lift it to your mouth. Pile the shells neatly on a side plate.

Oysters: if these come with a fork, treat them like mussels, above. Otherwise, eat straight from the shell: simply lift it up and tip the whole oyster into your mouth.

Pasta: should be eaten with a fork, except perhaps a lasagne, whose fork-resistant cheesy crust may need a knife too. No one over the age of six should be seen eating pasta with a spoon. With small forms of pasta such as ravioli or penne, using a fork should present no problem. With spaghetti, tagliatelle and the like, push the fork vertically into the pasta and twirl it to form a manageable mouthful. This requires some practice – it sounds easier than it is – and Her Ladyship confesses that,

Her Ladyship confesses that, in the far-distant days when she wore her hair long and loose, she largely gave up eating spaghetti.

in the far-distant days when she wore her hair long and loose, she largely gave up eating spaghetti. Long hair, unless it is firmly tied back, is compatible only with short pasta.

Pizza: even that bastion of correct form, Debrett's, now acknowledges that it is permissible to eat pizza with the fingers. But it warns against hunching over your food: 'Try to sit up straight, don't intrude into your neighbour's space and never put your elbows on the table.' Advice, Her Ladyship would add, that applies to eating any food on any occasion, with or without cutlery.

Prawns: if these are served in their shells, do as much of the peeling as possible with a knife and fork. Once that is done, and if a finger bowl is provided, you may safely assume that you have permission to use your fingers.

Snails: these are normally served in their shells, in a round dish with an indentation for each snail and with their own special cutlery. Hold the shell with the tongs, extract the snail with the fork and use that to lift it to your mouth. Once the snails are eaten, tear some bread into small pieces with your fingers and use it to mop up the garlic butter that almost certainly remains.

Finger bowls

Small bowls, half-filled with warm water and perhaps a slice of lemon, should be supplied with any food to be eaten with the fingers. The idea is that you dip your fingertips (not the whole hand) in the water before wiping them on your napkin. A smart restaurant or formal dinner will supply one bowl per person; in less formal settings a bowl may be shared between two or three, but should be conveniently positioned for all of them – it defeats the purpose of not dirtying napkins if instead you drip garlic butter over the tablecloth.

Chopsticks

The difficulty of eating with chopsticks if you are a novice surely explains why so many Chinese restaurants use paper tablecloths or, at the higher end of the scale, two linen cloths, the upper of which may be removed before pudding and coffee are served. Her Ladyship confesses to having left a trail of soy-soaked rice around her bowl on many an occasion before she mastered the technique.

She therefore advises a little rehearsal before attempting to use chopsticks in public. Rest one chopstick between the thumb and forefinger of your preferred hand and keep it steady with your middle and fourth fingers. Position the second chopstick parallel to it and grip it with your thumb, forefinger and middle finger. Keeping the first chopstick still, use the forefinger and middle finger (but not the thumb) to manipulate the second chopstick in a pincer movement. Pick up only a very small amount of food at a time and convey it to your mouth.

This is (with practice) both easier than it sounds and easier when the food is served in the small, high-sided bowls favoured by most Chinese and Vietnamese restaurants. Chinese people, it might be noted, hold the bowl under the mouth while eating to catch the inevitable spillages, but most Westerners cannot bring themselves to do this.

If the operation defeats you, Her Ladyship suggests you express a preference for Thai food. Not only will it sound sophisticated, but you can be secure in the knowledge that you will be provided with a spoon and fork. According to Thai etiquette the spoon rather than the fork should carry the food to the mouth, though Her Ladyship has observed that few people follow this tradition in her local restaurant.

In a Japanese restaurant, bear in mind that sushi is traditionally a finger food. Whether you choose to eat it with your fingers or with chopsticks, it should be done in one bite, or at most two, and not replaced on the plate between bites.

Many cultures perceive the left hand as dirty, for reasons Her Ladyship would prefer not to go into. If in any doubt at all, use your right hand for finger food.

The bill

It is Her Ladyship's view that if you are splitting the bill, you should split the bill. While, as mentioned above, she deplores those who order lavish dishes at someone else's expense, she has even less time for those who point out that they had only one glass of wine and didn't have a pudding. It is extraordinarily difficult to suggest that you should pay less without sounding either miserly or holier-than-thou.

While she deplores those who order lavish dishes at someone else's expense, she has even less time for those who point out that they had only one glass of wine and didn't have a pudding.

She recommends, therefore, that members of the group who have been extravagant should *offer* to pay more than those who have been restrained, rather than having this forced upon them by the parsimony of others. Offering to pay for the wine or to deal with the tip may make all the difference between keeping the temperate person happy and sending them home vowing never to have dinner with you again.

Tipping

A service charge is often included in a restaurant bill; if so, there is no obligation to add a further tip unless you feel the service has been spectacular. If a service charge has not been included, add on 12½–15 per cent of the total bill. Leaving the tip in cash makes it more likely that the money will go to your waiter rather than into the pockets of the management, although many modern credit-card machines make doing this unnecessarily complicated. It is up to you and your conscience whether you run the risk of short-changing your waiter or go away disgruntled at having been manoeuvred into leaving a tip on top of a service charge.

7

LESS FORMAL PARTIES

Strange to see how a good dinner and feasting reconciles everybody.

SAMUEL PEPYS, *DIARY*, 1665

This chapter takes a break from Her Ladyship's regal examples, as it deals with the sort of party to which most of her readers are unlikely to invite a member of the Royal family. She also feels it would be impertinent of her to give advice to any Royal on making conversation or remembering people's names: they have competent staff whose job it is to brief them in advance and avoid the embarrassment that absentmindedness or suddenly feeling inanely tongue-tied causes all too often.

The etiquette of invitations has been given in Chapter 5 and although it is less rigid for informal parties, the rules of basic good manners apply: if you are invited to something, you reply, rather than leaving your potential host wondering if you have left the country; if you have accepted, you turn up (and you don't turn up without accepting); you arrive and leave at the appointed times. In between times, you behave like a model guest: making an effort to talk to people you don't know; offering to help but backing off graciously if the host is happier on his or her own; praising the food; and not drinking so much that you become an embarrassment.

However casual the occasion, it is somewhat ungracious to arrive at a friend's house empty-handed. Flowers, chocolates or a bottle of wine are the most usual 'gesture presents', though Her Ladyship has a friend who is involved in the music business and frequently comes bearing a new CD. For a special occasion such as a birthday, anniversary or house-warming, something more substantial and personal is appropriate.

If you bring wine, don't expect it to be opened immediately: your host may already have chosen wine to complement the meal. If you are knowledgeable about wine and feel you know your host well enough, say, 'I wouldn't mind trying that, if it doesn't upset your plans', but don't insist if the host doesn't respond enthusiastically. It is a present, after all, and if you were that eager to taste it you should have bought an extra bottle and kept it at home.

A word of warning about flowers: avoid choosing a bunch that needs to be arranged straight away. Your host has other things to worry about. Buy a bouquet whose stems are already in water; they can then be put to one side and dealt with after dinner, or the next day. Or bring a potted plant instead.

Eating habits II

With a private dinner party it is permissible to tell your host – in advance – if you have strong dislikes. Indeed, a sensible host, inviting you for the first time, will ask if there is anything you don't eat. If she does, keep your list to one or two items. Her Ladyship has a substantial mental list of the friend who is allergic to prawns, the one who can't bear to have yoghurt even mentioned in her presence and, stretching the bounds of credulity, the one who doesn't like chocolate. But she knows that she can serve these people almost anything else and that they will appreciate it. She also has friends who will bring their own gluten-free bread or, if they are coming to stay, cereal: both of these are practical solutions to a dietary restriction. Someone who suffers from diabetes or is on a low-salt or low-fat diet for health reasons is entitled to have a longer list of foods they must avoid, but again polite guests should keep these to a minimum and accept that there will be occasions when they are offered foods that they have to refuse.

Most hosts can cater for vegetarians, but if you have omitted to give advance warning, apologise with the minimum of fuss and eat the vegetables. It is unreasonable to expect anyone other than a hired helper unexpectedly to whip up an omelette in the middle of a dinner party.

Managing your guest list

As host of a party in your own home, you have absolute discretion over whom you invite. It is, of course, only courteous to return hospitality, but you are still entitled to choose when and how you do this. Specifically, you are not obliged to invite anybody that you feel won't fit in to a certain gathering. Her Ladyship has one old friend whose new partner she finds sadly dreary; she chooses to invite this couple to dinner on their own, when the woman concerned may bore her but won't bore her friends, or to larger parties, at which the offender can be absorbed into the masses – she wouldn't inflict her on a dinner party of six or eight. She also has friends who hold (and have been known to express) strong political views that dominate the conversation; she doesn't invite them to the same small supper party as a meeker couple who might be overwhelmed. On the more positive side, she has several friends, both couples and singletons, whom she knows she can invite to meet absolutely anybody, because they are friendly, interesting and adept at making conversation flow. This sort of choice is entirely up to you as host, and requires only that you give some thought to the comfort of your guests.

An exception to this rule arises, however, if you live in a small community. If your neighbours can see who is coming to your house and you want to remain on good terms, you may sometimes feel obliged to explain to someone why you haven't included them in a certain gathering. The best way around this is to ask them for another date *before* mentioning the occasion to which they are not invited. For example, 'Could you come for lunch on the 18th?... Oh good, because Sheila and Paul are coming on the 11th, I owe Mary and Steve, and you know I can't cope with more than six... So I thought if you could come on the 18th I might invite Chris and Sam as well...' Unless the person you are speaking to can't stand Chris and Sam (and Her Ladyship hopes you will have had the tact to find this out in advance), this strategy should avoid any embarrassment or ill feeling.

One embarrassing situation that can't be avoided arises when couples split up acrimoniously. Friends who don't want to take sides will continue to invite both of them to small parties, separately and roughly turn and turn about. For larger occasions, such as a special birthday or even a wedding, the host is faced with a unpalatable choice: either invite one but not the other (unpleasant, but bearable if one of the former couple is a closer friend); or tell both of them that you are inviting the other and trust that they have the manners to be civil, or manage to avoid each other in a large gathering. As long as you have warned both parties in advance that the other will be present, you have done your duty; if they feel they can't bear to be in the same room as their ex, they may choose to stay away.

Avoiding undesirables

You can't be expected to like all the friends of all your friends, and at business parties even the host may not like all his or her guests. So there is always the risk that you are going to come across someone to whom you take an instant aversion. Or, indeed, the boring partner mentioned a few paragraphs ago.

At a dinner party at which you are seated next to this person, there is little you can do other than grit your teeth, try to change the subject, talk to the person on your other side or exert yourself to bring others into the conversation. If you happen to be placed next to someone whose attentions become personal, you are entitled firmly to remove a hand from your thigh and, as a last resort, to press the prongs of your fork into it.

You are entitled firmly to remove a hand from your thigh and, as a last resort, to press the prongs of your fork into it.

At a larger gathering when people are standing up and circulating, making an excuse to abandon a bore or other undesirable is easier: you can pretend to go to the loo, need another drink or spot someone to whom you simply *must* talk. Alternatively, fall back on the time-honoured, 'How very interesting, but please don't let me monopolise you.' Make sure, before you utter these words, that someone you know is within reach, tap them on the shoulder and introduce them before they have a chance to realise what is going on. Add something like, 'X has just been telling me all about his dried flower collection – I'm sure you'll be fascinated' and disappear. A word of warning, however: assuming that the newcomer cares as little as you do about dried flowers, this tactic could quickly lose you friends.

Overcoming shyness

A good host will always make sure that everyone has someone to talk to, but there may be times when he or she is preoccupied with answering the door or organising food. If you find yourself at a loss, ask your host if you can help by taking trays of canapés round or replenishing drinks: in Her Ladyship's experience, most people are pleased to see you if you have a tray or a bottle in your hand. If your host doesn't need help, he should at least recognise your plight and take a moment to introduce you to someone congenial. But even bearing in mind the warnings about bores and undesirables given above, there is no need to feel embarrassed about introducing yourself to a fellow guest in a friend's home.

Offering to help is not an option if there are staff, and at a large gathering it is easy to feel a bit bereft. If this happens to you, don't try to ingratiate yourself into an animated conversation. The people you are interrupting are likely to regard you as a sad annoyance rather than a welcome addition to their circle. Instead, remember that other people will be in the same boat: look around for someone on their own, go up, say hello and follow Her Ladyship's guidelines for conversation (see page 80). You will probably be putting them out of their misery just as they are putting you out of yours.

Forgetting names

This is something we are all prone to do, but Her Ladyship once observed a deft way of dealing with it. At a business-related drinks party she approached a client of long standing, who was talking to a distinguished-looking stranger. The client looked at her with great embarrassment and said, 'I'm terribly sorry, I've forgotten your name.' Her Ladyship automatically introduced herself and the stranger did the same.

Later, she took her client to task – they had, after all, been working together for some years.

'Yes, I know,' he said, 'but I couldn't remember the other man's name. I couldn't introduce *him* to *you*, so I had to get him to do it himself.'

This isn't going to work if the person whose name you pretend to have forgotten is your wife or best friend, but on the occasion in question it covered up any awkwardness.

Another friend of Her Ladyship, having recently moved to a small town, found herself frequently invited to drinks parties to meet a seemingly endless succession of local residents. She subsequently saw in the street a woman to whom she knew she had spoken at length two nights earlier.

'How are the cats?' she asked brightly. 'I hope they're feeling better. I'm really sorry, I don't remember your name, but I do remember the cats.'

No cat-lover is going to take offence at this 'honesty is the best policy' approach.

When neither of these devices is available to you, honesty is again the best policy: you can't introduce someone whose name you don't know, so simply apologise politely and confess that you have forgotten.

Some people recommend word association as a way of remembering names; Her Ladyship ventures to suggest that this option is not open to everyone. You may visualise a tree to help you remember the name of a Mr Birch, but it is surely even more embarrassing if your memory or arboricultural knowledge lets you down and you call him Mr Wood or Mr Beech.

8

CALLS AND VISITING

There are many people who proclaim, 'I always say what I think,',
but in nine cases out of ten they show that they have no consideration
for the feelings of others. LADY TROUBRIDGE, *THE BOOK OF ETIQUETTE* (1926)

Her Ladyship feels it is safe to assume that, even in these relaxed
times, few of her readers will receive an unexpected visit from
a member of the Royal Family, unless they are already well
acquainted. If they *are* entertaining Royalty, this fact takes
precedence over the usual forms of etiquette. Another guest
is presented (rather than 'being introduced') to the Royal,
regardless of the gender of either. The correct form of words
is 'Your Majesty (or Your Royal Highness), may I present….'

The 'morning call' used to be a mainstay of society and
involved its own complex etiquette about who should call on
whom first, whether they should simply leave cards (and if so
how many) or actually ask to see the lady of the house, how long
a visit should last and when and how it should be returned. Her
Ladyship is inclined to use the
word rigmarole rather than
etiquette here, and to be
grateful that it has largely
disappeared into the mists of
time. Nowadays she would say
that if somebody new moves

Her Ladyship is inclined to use
the word rigmarole rather than
etiquette here, and to be grateful
that it has largely disappeared
into the mists of time.

into your village, neighbourhood or block of flats, you should feel
free to drop in on them within a day or two of their arrival,

possibly bearing a home-made cake or some other treat they won't have had time to make for themselves lately.

A 'welcome to the neighbourhood' call should be brief unless you are sincerely urged to stay. The newcomers almost certainly have unpacking and arranging still to do. Indeed, if you drop in unannounced, you have no right to be offended if your new neighbour says apologetically, 'I can't even offer you tea: we haven't found the cups yet.'

Whether or not you make that first visit, there is no hierarchy governing how a relationship with new neighbours should develop.

If you like what you see of the new people, you may invite them for a drink or supper. Equally, the newcomers may invite you. Or not.

If you like what you see of the new people, you may invite them for a drink or supper, perhaps with other neighbours in order to help them feel at home. Equally, the newcomers may invite you. Or not. It obviously makes sense to be on friendly terms with your neighbours in case of domestic emergencies, difficulties over shared fences and having someone to feed the cat while you are away; it is also courteous to notify them if you are holding a party, having building works done or doing anything else that is going to disturb them. But there is no obligation for anyone to be bosom friends with the people who live next door or upstairs. Many of Her Ladyship's acquaintance are on what they consider perfectly friendly terms with their neighbours without ever doing more than saying hello in passing on the High Street or in the hallway.

Unexpected callers

A friend of Her Ladyship, living in the centre of London, sometimes receives a call from friends who are in town to visit an exhibition or renew their passports, suggesting that they might come round for coffee in an hour's time. Others, living farther from the Passport Office, hear from long-lost cousins who are 'just passing and thought we might drop in'. While this sort of surprise is often charming, it may also be utterly inconvenient. If the latter, you should not be embarrassed to say so. 'I'm really sorry, I'm going out in half an hour' or 'I've got a deadline to meet and I'm up to my eyes' are valid excuses and the spur-of-the-moment caller should accept them as such. In these circumstances, too, the expression 'take us as you find us' comes into its own: short-notice visitors cannot expect you to have cleared up your paperwork or put fresh flowers on the table, as you might have done if you had known they were coming. As an extreme example, Her Ladyship has one friend who drinks only herbal tea; although she keeps tea and coffee in the house she often has to ask impromptu callers to stop at the corner shop and buy milk.

Bringing this sort of visit to an end should be straightforward: self-invited guests should be sensitive to the fact that, however delighted you are to see them, you had probably set the time aside to do something else. They should respond promptly and cheerfully to remarks such as, 'I'm sorry, I'm going to have to throw you out – I must do some work' or 'The children will be

110

home any minute and I haven't finished X.' If they don't take the hint, start tidying up, checking emails or doing whatever else you have just suggested you should be doing. Ask pointed questions about train times or when their parking expires – only the truly pachydermous will fail to get the message.

Even if you have invited your guests, rather than allowing them to invite themselves, it can be tricky to make them go home. As Her Ladyship has mentioned elsewhere in this book, you should always make clear in an invitation – even a verbal one – what is included and what is not. If you want people to come for afternoon tea but not linger into the evening, tell them about your later commitment: 'I have to go out about seven, so if you come at four that would give us plenty of time for a gossip before I have to get changed' or 'The children are at their grandmother's all afternoon, so I am free until six' sets the ground rules without making you appear inhospitable. The same applies if you are inviting people for the weekend: 'I hope you can stay for Sunday lunch' clearly implies that you don't expect your guests to stay for supper – or even afternoon tea.

Even if you have invited your guests, rather than allowing them to invite themselves, it can be tricky to make them go home.

If you are the guest in circumstances such as these, Her Ladyship would refer you once more to some wise words from Lady Troubridge:

There are many people who do not know when to depart, and simply because they are afraid of leaving too early and offending the hostess, they prolong the visit until their hostess is scarcely able to stifle her yawns.

Her Ladyship very much hopes that her readers have more *savoir faire* than that.

Staying the night

Not everyone has an endless supply of spare bed linen and duvets, so if you are travelling by car and a bit more luggage is no problem, it is a friendly gesture to offer to bring your own. It also means that it is you rather than your host who is burdened with the extra laundry. One friend of Her Ladyship, an academic who routinely has two months off in the summer, moved to a particularly pretty part of the West Country and found that different sets of friends and relations invited themselves for a few days each throughout her first long vacation. 'I was supposed to be getting on with my research,' she complained later, 'but I seemed to do nothing but change sheets and re-make beds.'

Remember, too, that not everyone has an endless supply of hot water. A thoughtful host will ask you if you want a bath or shower in the morning or if you prefer to have one before you retire; he or she will also warn you of any idiosyncrasies of the shower mechanism or hot-water system. If not, check that your preferred routine fits in with theirs, and don't fill the bath to the brim, leaving others to endure lukewarm ablutions.

Dogs

The important thing to remember about dogs is that not everyone loves them. If you are invited somewhere where your host doesn't want you to bring your dog, that is an end of the matter: he or she is under no obligation to provide an excuse and you have no right to insist, whatever you think of their attitude. Find a reliable kennels or dog-sitter so that you can, when you have to, go away and leave your dog behind.

If, as a dog-owner, you invite non-dog-owners to your home, you can, up to a point, expect them to put up with your pet. But

Being the perfect guest

Everybody has their own house rules, even if they are not aware of them all. Many people always sit in the same armchair and will be irritated if you occupy their spot; others like everyone to take their shoes off the moment they come in the door. To an outsider this may seem petty; to the host it may make all the difference between enjoying a guest's company and being desperate for them to go away. A friend of Her Ladyship once went to stay with her brother for a week and, after four days, was surprised to be chastised for not rubbing the shower down with a scraper every morning after she had used it. 'How was I to know? You didn't tell me,' was her not unreasonable response.

While you shouldn't, of course, expect to be waited on hand and foot in a friend's house (unless there is an army of servants to pander to your every whim), you should be sensitive to the fact that they might *prefer* to wait on you. If your hosts respond to your repeated offers of help with a polite 'No, I'm fine, thanks – you go and read the paper', take them at their word. Some people are uncomfortable with anyone else hovering around their kitchen; others genuinely enjoy pampering their guests.

Her Ladyship's advice is: if you are the host, make your guests aware at the outset of anything you feel strongly about, rather than enduring their misdemeanours with ever-increasing annoyance; if you are the guest, be sensitive to such details as those mentioned above, ask if in doubt and listen carefully for the sound of gritted teeth.

only up to a point. A boisterous dog that tears guests' stockings or causes them to spill drinks should be excluded from the room for the duration of the visit, and should also be kept out of the way of anyone who is unsteady on their feet or seems to be frightened. Just because you know that backing away and waving your hands is a way of encouraging your dog to play, it doesn't mean that your guests are familiar with your training regime.

Guests staying overnight have the right to be free of dogs in their bedroom, unless they specifically and enthusiastically request otherwise. Her Ladyship has friends who own an exuberant Sheltie and weekend visits to their home always means early morning doggy greetings. As it happens, Her Ladyship loves this and her friends know it; if she objected she could shut her bedroom door more firmly –

Her Ladyship's attitude would be very different if her friends owned a Labrador.

and she has to acknowledge that this dog weighs perhaps 6kg (13lb) and is particularly light on its feet. Her Ladyship's attitude would be very different if her friends owned a Labrador.

When to go home

As Her Ladyship mentioned earlier in this chapter, an invitation to stay should make it clear when the hosts expect the guests to go home. But it is also up to the guests to behave with sensitivity. Her Ladyship has one friend who lives close to a major airport and is often asked for accommodation the night before a flight. As soon as the travellers arrive, he enquires, jokingly and with much light-hearted apology, when they are planning to leave. This is not because he is inhospitable – on the contrary – but because he has his own life to lead. There is, after all, a wealth of difference between a flight at 6pm (check-in at 3pm, leave his house just after lunch) and one at 10pm (check-in at 7pm, stay all afternoon and possibly hope for an early supper), yet both could equally accurately be described as 'an evening flight' by someone who didn't have to worry about the catering.

Your host's domestic circumstances will also give you an idea of how convenient or otherwise your visit is. If the spare bedroom doubles as a home office – as many do – it is tactful to vacate it well before Monday morning, when its usual occupant is likely to want to go back to work. Similarly, if you know that you are sleeping in the bedroom of one of the children and that the evicted child is either on the sofa or in its parents' bed, there is a strong likelihood that everyone will be fed up after a couple of nights. Not for nothing did Benjamin Franklin observe that 'fish and visitors smell in three days'. He also, by the way, remarked that 'three may keep a secret, if two of them are dead' – a pithy endorsement of Her Ladyship's remarks on chocolate teapots (see page 83).

9

RITES OF PASSAGE

If it were not for the presents, an elopement would be preferable.

GEORGE ADE, *FORTY MODERN FABLES* (1901)

As with Royal Garden Parties, if you are fortunate enough to be invited to a Royal wedding your invitation will include information on dress and timing. The wedding of the future Duke and Duchess of Cambridge, like all Royal occasions, was a masterpiece of planning, with the principals' arrivals at Westminster Abbey timed to the minute.

The seating plan in the Abbey was also carefully arranged, with the Royal Family sitting to the right of aisle (the traditional place for the groom's relations), and foreign Royals and invited Members of Parliament behind them; on the left were the bride's family, the couple's close friends and members of the groom's mother's family. The general congregation was further back, away from the centre of things, as would be the case with non-family members in many formal but less illustrious weddings.

Many bridegrooms – and indeed some brides – would sympathise with Mr Ade's point of view, quoted above, for a lot of fuss *is* made about weddings. People who have never given the matter a thought are required to have opinions on the colour of bridesmaids' dresses, the correct style of waistcoat and who should sit with whom on which table; they can be forgiven for wishing that it was all over. Despite the petty irritations, however, for many people their wedding day is the one occasion in their lives when they really want to 'do it right'.

A general rule that has served Her Ladyship well is that the more formal the occasion, the more rigidly you should stick to the 'rules'. If you are nervous about the 'right' way to go about things, you can gain confidence from following in the footsteps of generations of party givers and wedding planners.

Wedding invitations

There used to be an accepted form for wedding invitations:
Mrs and Mr Geoffrey Edmonds request the pleasure of your company at the marriage of their daughter Joanna to Mr Patrick Travers on such and-such-a-date at this time and place. The bride's surname was not mentioned because it was assumed to be the same as her parents'.

The invitation was phrased in this way because the bride's parents traditionally paid for the wedding and were therefore considered the hosts. It was also the rule rather than the exception that the bride's parents were still married to each other at the time of their daughter's nuptials. Nowadays there are many other variables to be taken into account.

If the bride's parents are no longer together but are jointly paying for the wedding, the invitation should come from Mr Geoffrey Edmonds and Mrs Carmen Edmonds, if the mother has not remarried, or Mr Geoffrey Edmonds and Mrs Steven Blackstone, if she has. If the bride's natural father is not involved but her stepfather is, the invitation should come from Mr and Mrs Steven Blackstone and refer to the marriage of *her* daughter. In these circumstances and to avoid confusion it is sensible to include the bride's surname.

Older couples or those who have been together a long time may choose to host their own wedding, in which case the invitation comes from them both and dispenses with the prefixes: *Joanna Edmonds and Patrick Travers* (or *Jo Edmonds and Pat Travers*, if that is how they prefer to be known) *request the pleasure...*

Whatever the form of the invitation, it should include the request to 'RSVP' (short for *répondez s'il vous plaît*, which is French for 'please reply') by a certain date and give the name and address of the person to whom the acceptance or refusal should be sent.

Sending wedding invitations six weeks in advance used to be the norm; most people would now think that was ridiculously late and that something nearer six months gives more room for manoeuvre. Many invitation lists include aunts, uncles and old friends of the family who 'have' to be asked but are unlikely to accept because they are too frail to travel or because

It is sensible to have a back-up list of people to invite and to leave sufficient time for those on this B list not to feel they have been crammed in at the last minute.

they live in Brazil. This is one reason for putting a 'please reply by' date on the invitation: it is sensible to have a back-up list of people to invite should the aunt in Brazil decline and to leave sufficient time for those on this B list not to feel they have been crammed in at the last minute.

Everyone knows that weddings are expensive and that numbers have to be limited, so no one should be offended at not being invited. Nevertheless, a little consideration can help ease any possible hurt. Many years ago, a close friend of Her Ladyship became engaged to a man with a large family. When the wedding invitations were sent out, the friend said, 'We'd love to invite you, but Jeremy has so many cousins... You're right at the top of our reserve list.' Whether or not this was true Her Ladyship has no way of knowing; on that occasion all the cousins (and perhaps also the aunt from Brazil) did attend and Her Ladyship did not. But it was impossible to be other than touched by this consummate display of tact on the part of the bride.

The rule that invitations should make it clear what is included in the invitation is never more true than with weddings. Many couples invite only close friends and family to the ceremony and to a sit-down meal immediately afterwards, then ask more people to a less formal party in the evening. Decisions as to who should be invited to what are dictated by budget, the size of the room, the number of aunts in Brazil and other such factors, as well as the bride and groom's wishes, and it is impossible to lay down hard and fast rules about this. The one thing that is not acceptable is to invite someone to an early part of the day's proceedings but not to the later: in other words, you can ask people not to come before an appointed hour, but you can't tell *You can ask people not to come before an appointed hour, but you can't tell them when to go home.* them when to go home, unless it is the official end of the party and everyone else is leaving too. Elderly grandmothers may choose to make their excuses when the party becomes too loud for them, in which case a taxi or other escort home should be organised. But if they prefer to stay and join in the revelry until two in the morning, that is up to them.

Steps and exes

It has been well said that the difficulty of coping with the bride and groom's re-married parents 'can turn a wedding invitation list into a social tinderbox'. Much obviously depends on how well all concerned get on (or are prepared to pretend to get on for the duration of the wedding) and how long the new partner has been in the bride or groom's life. A stepfather who married the bride's mother when the bride was two after her natural father had disappeared is a very different creature from one who has come on the scene only recently and was responsible for the break-up of the first marriage.

It is up to the bride who she chooses to give her away. Traditionally this is her father, but she may prefer her stepfather if he has played a more significant role in her life. Under these circumstances she may ask her natural father to make a speech at the reception or give a reading during the service. Or she may reverse these functions, asking her natural father to give her away and giving her stepfather some other important part to play.

Parents' long-term partners should be invited, but not treated as part of the wedding party. The parents of both bride and groom sit at the top table during the reception; if some or all are remarried, their spouses could be allocated to the second table, along with, perhaps, the partners of the best man and bridesmaids. This is obviously not advisable if putting these people on the same table is likely to cause a scene. In that case, allocate each one an escort for the day – perhaps a sibling of the bride or groom or an unmarried aunt or uncle – so that no one is made to feel they are in a social wilderness.

Children at weddings

Tradition has it that the wedding day 'belongs' to the bride and should be arranged according to her wishes. Nowadays most people would feel that the groom's feelings should also be taken into account, but in any case it is entirely up to the couple whether or not children are invited. If the bride invites small nieces and nephews or the children of close friends to be her attendants, she cannot decently exclude any siblings of those attendants, but other than that she is under no obligation. It is up to the parents of uninvited children to arrange for childcare and accept the invitation, or to decline on the basis that spending time with their children takes precedence. The gracious bride will disguise her disappointment (or her relief) if the latter is the decision.

> *However central to your personal universe your children may be, they are not the stars of this particular show.*

If children are invited, parents must ensure that they behave and are not allowed to run riot through church or reception. Crying babies should be taken outside and soothed rather than allowed to interrupt the ceremony. However central to your personal universe your children may be, they are not the stars of this particular show.

Presents

If you are attending a wedding, you should take or send a present; if you have been invited but cannot attend sending a present is not obligatory, but will be seen as a thoughtful gesture.

The most practical way to manage the selection of wedding presents is for the bride and groom to set up a list at one of the many shops offering this service. Not only does this ensure that they receive presents they actually want (and not the six toast-racks that were once a cliché of the bridegroom's speech), it makes it possible for givers to shop online and arrange to have the gift delivered directly to the address specified by the bride and groom.

Those who find this a touch impersonal can go to the shop, inspect the list, choose, purchase, wrap and deliver their present themselves – as long as they inform the department in charge of the wedding list that they have bought a particular item.

When setting up a list of desired presents, the bride and groom should bear in mind the donors' varying budgets. The less well-heeled members of your circle should not be made to feel uncomfortable – or miserly – if they can afford no more than a plate or two of the lavish dinner service on which you have set your heart.

If, as a guest, you are physically taking your gift with you on the day, keep it with you during the ceremony: there is likely to be a table at the entrance to the reception where presents are to be left. If in doubt, ask the best man, one of the ushers or a member of staff at the reception venue.

It used to be considered bad form for the bride and groom to ask for money, but this is increasingly common – and very practical, given that they are likely already to be living together and to own the sort of things traditionally given as wedding presents. Her Ladyship sees no objection to their preferring a contribution to 'the honeymoon of a lifetime'. One couple of her acquaintance, well into their forties and about to embark on a second marriage for both of them, included a note in their invitation explaining that they had fallen in love with a particularly expensive dining table and would welcome financial assistance towards buying it: after all, they managed to convey with great delicacy, they already had a houseful of bed linen and cutlery, they really didn't need any more. Unconventional, perhaps, but surely preferable to allowing family and friends to waste their money on unwanted gifts. A year or so later, Her Ladyship visited the couple in question and was delighted to be told that she had made a contribution to the elegant table at which they dined.

It used to be considered bad form for the bride and groom to ask for money, but this is increasingly common – and very practical.

Whatever form your gift takes, make sure it is accompanied by a card with your name written legibly on it. The bride and groom will be embarrassed – and you, as the giver, may well be offended – if they don't know whom to thank.

Thank-you letters should be written – preferably by hand (see page 142) as soon as possible after the return from honeymoon, or within a few days of the wedding if the honeymoon is not to be taken immediately. Traditionally the bride wrote to thank those on the groom's side and vice versa; many couples now choose to write in both their names. The important thing is to make the letters personal: thank the giver for coming to the wedding and helping to make the day so special, but also for the specific gift, making reference to the pleasure it will give. Something along the lines of 'We hope to be doing a lot of entertaining, so your lovely champagne glasses will be christened very shortly' or 'We have both always longed to travel round South America, and your generous cheque brings us a step closer' will make the recipients feel their offering has been appreciated, rather than lost under a deluge of wrapping paper.

Note that it is not necessary for guests to write letters of thanks after a wedding.

Photography

Almost everyone employs a professional photographer and/or video-maker to record their wedding day. His or her needs *must* take precedence over any snaps guests wish to take. It is usual for the professional to take a series of group shots: bride and groom together, with and without attendants and parents; groom, best man and ushers together; and so on. It would be the height of rudeness for an amateur armed with a smartphone to interfere with the flow of this, asking the subjects to 'hang on a minute' in order to take a picture of their own. Curb your enthusiasm, take impromptu pictures without disturbing anyone and, if you wish, order more formal ones from the photographer in due course. You should also never take photographs inside a church without the vicar's permission, nor distract everyone's attention during the service by using a flash.

Logistics

If a wedding reception is to be held at any distance from
the service itself, arrangements are usually made to ensure
that all the guests can get there. This may range from
simply asking X to give Y a lift to hiring a double-decker
bus to convey everyone. If you know that you are going to
need transport and can't make a private arrangement with
one of the other guests, let someone – probably the mother
of the bride or the best man – know in advance so that they
can organise something for you.

At christenings and funerals these arrangements may
be more ad hoc, but there should always be someone
checking that everyone knows where they are going and
has the means of getting there. If you are driving and have
space in your car, make a point of not setting off until you
are sure no one is going to be left stranded.

Speeches

At the meal or party following the wedding ceremony, the best
man generally acts as master of ceremonies and begins by inviting
the bride's father – or, in his absence, her stepfather, uncle,
godfather or other close male connection – to speak. This speech
is always a fond tribute to the bride and ends with a toast to the
bride and groom. The groom replies to this toast, thanks his new
in-laws for hosting such a splendid occasion (if they have done so)
and for allowing him to marry their wonderful daughter (ditto).

He also thanks everyone who has been involved in organising the day, including the guests for coming, and ends by proposing a toast to the bridesmaids. The best man replies on behalf of the bridesmaids, reminisces about the youthful indiscretions of the groom (now firmly behind him) and reads any important or witty messages from those who have been unable to attend. The tone of all these speeches should be light-hearted, affectionate and, if possible, amusing without being

The tone of all these speeches should be light-hearted, affectionate and, if possible, amusing without being ribald. Above all they should be short.

During the service

Many people never go to church except for weddings, christenings and funerals; increasingly you may be invited to the wedding of a friend from a different religious or cultural background. Whatever your beliefs or lack of them, it is a basic courtesy to respect the rituals of others. Bow your head, stand, sit or kneel when everyone else does: whoever is conducting the ceremony will normally tell you what to do and for a Christian church wedding the words 'the congregation will stand/sit' are often printed in the order of service. If no such guidance is given, copy your neighbour. If you don't know the hymns, mouth the words, mutter them quietly or stand in respectful silence. It is the height of bad manners to talk or, worse, giggle, at any point during a religious service of any kind.

ribald. Above all they should be short, so that the cake may be cut, passed round and eaten, the ceremonial side of the day may be considered over and the party can begin.

Although this was once the point at which the bride and groom set off for their honeymoon, this adherence to tradition has become the exception to the rule. Most newlyweds now prefer to stay, enjoy the party and revel in the fact that so many of their close friends and family are together in the same room, wishing them well. Traditionalists may frown on this; Her Ladyship says, 'Let them frown.' She fails to see why extending your enjoyment of your own wedding day should be considered a breach of etiquette.

Christenings

These may take place in the course of a regular Sunday church service or at a special time of their own, most commonly a Saturday. Unless you have reason to believe that the occasion will be very smart, dress should be one step up from smart casual (see page 64). There is no need to wear a hat, unless you are the sort of person who habitually wears a hat to church.

In the Church of England it is traditional for a boy baby to have two godfathers and one godmother, and a girl two godmothers and a godfather, but even traditions may change: this modest number may become

This modest number may become unfashionable since Prince George of Cambridge was blessed with seven godparents.

unfashionable since Prince George of Cambridge was blessed with seven godparents. Godparents are usually close friends or relations of the baby's parents, although Her Ladyship feels that inviting someone as close as a sister to be a godmother is a waste of an opportunity. A godparent is an *additional* special person in the life of the newborn and it seems pointless to confer this honour (and responsibility) on someone who is a near relative already.

Christians believe that godparents should have a strong religious faith, because they are considered responsible for the baby's spiritual welfare. Nowadays, many people are inclined to choose those who would be able and willing to look after the baby's worldly welfare should anything happen to the parents.

After the christening, it is usual to hold a small party to which family, close friends and the celebrant are invited. This may be lunch, tea or drinks, depending on the time of day. There are no particular rules about it, except that if the baby's parents have saved the top tier of their wedding cake for a special occasion, now is the time to cut it.

If you are invited to a christening, whether as a godparent or as an interested bystander, you should bring the baby a present, which should be of a permanent nature: silver spoons and mugs are the most traditional, but silver or jewellery of any kind is always acceptable. So are christening bibles and prayer books, providing the parents are believers and the baby is likely to be raised in the Christian faith. Another possibility is to open a savings account in the child's name, though this is probably better done after consultation with the parents; if they have had the same idea they may prefer a cheque so that they can keep all the baby's accumulating wealth in one account. If this seems too clinical, a block of premium bonds has the bonus of offering the (slight) prospect of great riches. Alternatively, consider a quantity of port, claret or other wine that the 'baby' can enjoy on his or her eighteenth birthday.

Baby names – the Royal Aspect

At the risk of sounding impertinent by expressing an opinion on something that is no concern of hers, Her Ladyship would like to congratulate their Royal Highnesses the Duke and Duchess of Cambridge on giving their first baby appropriately royal names. In her view, far too many celebrities saddle their children with the names of fruit or, worse, of the place where they were conceived or born. Names that seem 'cute' or 'adorable' for babes in arms and pretty toddlers can be a real burden in later years. And given the cringing embarrassment almost everyone feels on the subject of their parents having sex, it is brutal to force a child to be reminded of this intimate act every time someone addresses him or her by name. So please, Her Ladyship beseeches, fewer Apricots and Manhattans, more George Alexander Louis.

She also feels it is appropriate to utter a word of praise to the parents of the film director Duncan Jones. Having endured the early years of his life being known as Zowie (and later Joey) Bowie, he was able to revert to his real name as a young man. It helps, of course, that David Bowie was born with the surprisingly ordinary name of Jones, but Her Ladyship nevertheless applauds these decidedly unconventional parents' thinking to give their son a conventional first name. As a parent, it is worth remembering that however wacky, hip or convention-defying you are in your twenties and thirties, your children may grow up to be lawyers, accountants or indeed film directors: give them at least a fallback position.

Funerals

These vary so much with the individual occasion that it is difficult to give precise advice. Invitations are not generally sent out: you hear about the details of time and place either through an intimation in the newspaper or by word of mouth.

Even dress codes vary: for a traditional funeral in a church black is still the most appropriate. Men should wear a suit with a black tie, or at least one of unobtrusive colour and pattern. Women may choose a dress or smart suit; a hat is optional but will not be out of place (and of course in some cultures it is considered respectful to cover your head on these occasions). In a crematorium any subdued colour is acceptable, but hats run the risk of looking melodramatic.

However, if the family has decided that the funeral is not the mourning of a death but the celebration of a life, or if you are attending a memorial service some weeks or months after the death, rather than a funeral in its immediate aftermath, they may specifically request non-sombre clothing. If so, their wishes must be regarded as paramount. In such a case a lightly coloured dress or suit would be a good choice for women, with no flamboyant jewellery or accessories. Men should wear a suit, or at least a jacket and tie. Photography is not appropriate during a funeral service.

It is usual nowadays for only the family to send flowers, though if the deceased belonged to a club or professional body, or was a long-serving employee of a company, these establishments may send flowers or a wreath in the name of all the members or staff. As an alternative, donations to a charity connected to the deceased's last illness or to the hospice where he or she spent his/her last days are often requested. Send a cheque payable to the charity care of the funeral director, or send it direct to the charity; in either case include a covering note giving the name of the deceased. If there has been no mention of a charity in either a newspaper announcement or on the funeral order of service, don't be embarrassed to ask a member of the family or the funeral director if there are any special requests. If not, you may like to make a donation to a charity of your own choosing.

After a funeral or memorial, a party may be arranged at the home of the deceased or one of his or her family, or sandwiches provided at a local pub or village hall. While it may seem important on this occasion to have a word with the deceased's partner or children to express your condolences in person, bear in mind that all the other guests are likely to be doing the same thing and that funerals are often an ordeal for the bereaved, who are trying hard to put on a brave face for a few hours. It may sometimes be tactful just to sneak away and phone a few days later to let them know that they are in your thoughts.

10

DATING

Courtship consists in a number of quiet attentions, not so pointed as to alarm, nor so vague as not to be understood.

LAURENCE STERNE (1713–68)

The question of a modern Royal 'dating' is a vexed one because, as with anything else they do, they are likely to find their photographs plastered all over the papers. All too often these will be accompanied by coy captions referring to a Royal's 'mystery companion' and using words such as 'frolicking' if they happen to be photographed embracing, particularly on a beach or yacht.

For the rest of the world, dating is easier than it used to be. There have, of recent years, been big changes in its etiquette and this is good news for the modern female: she is no longer obliged to wait to be asked out. It is perfectly acceptable for a woman to ask a man if he would care to go for a drink sometime or, if this seems too forward, to include him in an outing with other friends or in a supper party she is giving. A man may accept this sort of invitation without feeling that he is committing himself to a serious relationship; if he wishes, he may subsequently reciprocate with an invitation of his own.

Asking someone out

There are two ways of doing this: the specific and the vague. The specific is, 'I have tickets for such-and-such on Friday week.

Would you like to come?' The vague is, 'Would you like to have a drink some time?'

Both have their advantages and disadvantages. The recipient of the specific invitation cannot be sure if the other party is 'asking them out' as a prelude to something more long-term or if they are simply looking for a companion for that one occasion. It behoves the asker to make this clear: 'My girlfriend's away for the weekend and I wondered if you'd like to come instead' should indicate that the offer is a one-off with no ulterior motive. On the other hand, 'It would be great if we could go together' is plainly more personal.

Someone who would like to go out with you but isn't free on Friday week (or isn't interested in the entertainment on offer) should not only decline with regret but create an opportunity for another invitation: 'I'd love to, but I'm not free that night. Do ask me another time' or 'Perhaps we could have a drink one evening' keeps the lines of communication open.

If you don't want to go out with someone, turning down a specific invitation is straightforward: 'I'm sorry, I can't on Friday' is all that needs to be said. If the inviter then comes up with 'What about Saturday?', it is easy to say that you are busy that day too. And so on, until the unwanted admirer finally picks up on the subtext of what you are saying. Beware, however, of putting off someone you don't want to discourage: a friend of Her Ladyship, asked out by an attractive casual acquaintance whose phone number she didn't have, told him that she was very busy for the next two weeks and asked if he would mind calling her after that. This was no prevarication – she was preparing for a major presentation and was temporarily working long hours. He, unfortunately, took it as a rejection and never contacted her again.

Accepting a vague invitation is also straightforward: 'That would be lovely. When are you free?' leads to a comparing of diary commitments and a date. It is turning down the vague invitation that can be difficult, because it means 'No, I really do not want to go out with you, under any circumstances' and is almost bound to be hurtful. Nonetheless, it has to be done. You are under no obligation to accept even one invitation from someone in whom you are not interested – and it would be cruel to give him or her false encouragement. Say, kindly but firmly, 'No, I don't think so, thank you.' By all means make yourself sound busier than you are if you think it will soften the blow, but keep your excuses vague: if you plead a demanding period at work or a friend from Australia staying, you will have to invent another excuse when your rejected suitor tries again in a few weeks' time.

Who pays?

If you have asked someone out for the first time – and this applies whether you are male or female, straight or gay – you should expect to make the arrangements and pay the bill. If you are the guest you should offer to pay your share but expect the offer to be refused. It would normally be rude to insist. The exception to that rule may be if you are not and are never going to be romantically interested in your companion and feel that accepting their generosity is going to put you under uncomfortable pressure. You are, of course, never obliged to go to bed with someone just because they have taken you out to dinner, but you may avoid embarrassment if you don't feel you 'owe' them anything.

A walk in the park with a picnic into which you have put imagination and effort can be every bit as meaningful as an expensive trip to the opera.

As a relationship progresses the question of who pays becomes less prickly. You fall into the habit of going Dutch, or of taking it in turns, with one of you sometimes treating the other for a special occasion or celebration. If one of you earns appreciably more than the other, it makes sense for him or her to bear the brunt of expenses on dates, without making the other half feel they are being patronised or that they are sponging. If you are the one who is short of money, make up for this by suggesting things to do that are charming without being costly: a walk in the park with a picnic into which you have put imagination and effort can be every bit as meaningful as an expensive trip to the opera.

Where to go

On a first date, you are sounding each other out. The person who has taken the initiative may be sure that he or she wants to pursue a relationship, but still needs to get to know the other person: the fluttery girlish charm that seemed so tantalising from a distance may turn out to be an irritating inability to make a decision.

Put some thought into where you go. Sitting opposite each other in a restaurant puts you under pressure to talk all the time; sitting in the dark in a theatre, cinema or concert hall means you can't talk at all and can raise embarrassing questions about whether or not to make physical contact. Instead, Her Ladyship advises going somewhere where dialogue is easy and permissible but need not be non-stop. An art gallery, a sporting fixture, a visit to the zoo may all be appropriate if you know that this is a shared interest; not only is there something to watch which will fill in any lulls in the conversation, but you will have something to discuss if you go for a drink or a meal afterwards.

Give conversation a chance to blossom, though. If you do decide to go to a bar or restaurant, choose one that isn't so noisy that you both spend most of the time saying, 'I'm sorry. What did you say?' There are few things, in Her Ladyship's opinion, more likely to make a relationship stumble at the first hurdle than having constantly to ask a companion to repeat what turn out to be conversational commonplaces.

Don't, on a first date, suggest going somewhere you have never been before. You want things to go smoothly, not waste half an hour looking for a parking space or find yourselves in a disappointing and overpriced restaurant that will put you both on edge.

Give some thought, too, to what to wear. If you are going out straight from work you may have little choice, but make sure that your hair is tidy, your hands and teeth are clean and, if appropriate, freshen your make-up. Otherwise, make it obvious that you have made a bit of effort – iron your shirt, clean your shoes and don't wear a jumper with a hole worn through the elbow. Be careful not to overdo it, though: too smart or 'dolled up' can be every bit as off-putting as too scruffy. Women should be wary of anything too revealing on a first date: like too much noise, too much cleavage can be a hindrance to conversation.

Daytime or early evening is best for a first date, as it is easier to escape if it really doesn't work out. If, for example, you meet in a bar after work, you can prepare an excuse for leaving after two drinks – and omit to use it if you are enjoying yourself. Many nervous daters ask a friend to ring them three-quarters of an hour after the time fixed for the meeting, giving them the opportunity to say to their date, 'I'm sorry, something's come up, I just have to go' if things are going disastrously, or to reassure their friend that all is well.

Wherever you go, try to be on time. If you are going to be more than a very few minutes late, phone or text *before* the appointed time to give an indication of when you expect to arrive. Many women still find it uncomfortable to sit in a pub or bar on their own, so if that is where you have arranged to meet it is all the more important for the man to be punctual (and sensible for a woman to have a book or newspaper to occupy her during those awkward spare minutes).

Mention of 'two drinks' reminds Her Ladyship of an important point: particularly on a first date, be realistic about the amount you can sensibly drink on an empty stomach. It is all too easy, after a glass or two, to find the person you are with more attractive than you might otherwise have done and to give him or her ill-considered encouragement. If you don't want either to cut the date short or to commit to prolonging the evening by going for a meal, switch to soft drinks or, at the very least, order a bag or two of crisps or peanuts if you feel that the effects of alcohol may be sneaking up on you.

At the end of the evening

Assuming that, at the end of the evening, you are going your separate ways, it is polite for a man to see a woman into a taxi or at least escort her to a stop or station and wait until she is safely on the bus or train. Offering to see a girl home, unless you live very close by, may be seen as predatory: it is too easy to claim that you have missed the last bus and will have to stay.

Her Ladyship believes that this is one occasion on which old-fashioned chivalry holds good: even if the man has paid for everything, he should still thank his companion for a lovely evening. She, in turn, should telephone, text or email the next day to thank him. If she is keen to pursue the relationship, she is at liberty to say, 'We must do that again some time' or even something more definite such as 'Would you like to go for a meal next week?' Thereafter, Her Ladyship hopes, nature may be left to take its course.

If, however, a woman feels that one date with this man has been one date too many, she should omit any suggestion, however vague, that they should ever meet again and hope that he gets the message.

Her Ladyship apologises for the gender-specific pronouns in the preceding paragraphs and assures her readers that these may be reversed or adapted to suit any similar situation.

Internet dating

Once upon a time a blind date was someone your friends 'set you up' with; nowadays it is more and more common to go out with someone you have 'met' only on line. A recent advertising campaign in London, warning against unlicensed minicabs, used the slogan, 'If it isn't booked, it's just a stranger's car' and Her Ladyship feels that this stern admonition applies equally well to internet dating: if you don't have friends in common, it's just a stranger. It is, as anyone who pays any attention to the news knows, horrifically easy to lie over the internet and to disguise even one's true age and gender, never mind one's personal peculiarities.

When you sign up for an internet dating site, take care over your profile and project the qualities that are important to you: if you lie about yourself and what you are looking for, you are likely to find a match for the lie rather than for the real you. When you contact someone, make it personal – mention something in their profile that attracted you. Don't be frightened to take the initiative: after all, you have taken a bold step by signing on to the site; there's no point in sitting passively waiting for people to contact you. And remember that the point of online dating is to meet people in the flesh. After a few friendly exchanges that make you feel you like this person, suggest a date and follow the guidelines for any other first date offered above.

Remember that the point of online dating is to meet people in the flesh. After a few friendly exchanges that make you feel you like this person, suggest a date.

This is, of course, the moment when you should remember that your new online friend is a stranger. Make the first date in a public place and tell someone where you are going. Make sure your phone is charged so that you can make contact with the outside world in an emergency. Her Ladyship would advise against going back to the date's home on a first date; if you decide to, phone a friend or relation, tell them what you are doing and ask them to phone you in half an hour. There is no need to be embarrassed about doing this in front of your date: you are every bit as much a stranger to him as he is to you and he should, if he is sensible, have taken similar precautions.

If, after a date or two, you feel you want to pursue a relationship with someone you have met online, invite him or her to meet a close friend or two. It can do no harm to have a second opinion, particularly from someone who has your best interests at heart. Then, if all seems to be well, relax and enjoy yourself.

11

COMMUNICATION

We already know that anonymous letters are despicable. In etiquette, as well as in law, hiring a hit man to do the job does not relieve you of responsibility. JUDITH MARTIN, 'MISS MANNERS' (BORN 1938)

The British Monarchy has an informative website (www.royal.gov.uk), a Facebook page with almost a million 'likes', and a Twitter account (@britishmonarchy) which gives the latest news on Royal events. It has even been known to retweet, passing on expressions of excitement from those whom a Royal is about to visit. Those who have fallen foul of libel laws or public vilification could learn something from studying the common-sense approach of the Monarchy's posts and tweets.

Her Ladyship mentioned earlier in this book that the formality of a response should match the formality of an invitation. In the etiquette of communication, much the same applies. It is a good axiom never to reply by email to anything that has not been sent by email. Although the personal handwritten letter, preferably using a fountain pen rather than a ballpoint or felt-tip, is in many walks of life a dying (or dead) art, it still has its place and is, in Her Ladyship's view, essential in one context and highly desirable in another (see page 142). The essential is the letter of condolence.

Condolence

Too many people avoid sending letters of condolence because, they say, 'I didn't know what to write.' To these, Her Ladyship would reply firmly, 'It is not about you.' At times of loss, letters and cards arriving in the post can provide a surprising amount of comfort and often become treasured keepsakes. In many ways it doesn't matter what you write – the important thing is to write *something* to indicate that you share the person's sense of loss. This applies equally if you knew the deceased but not his or her family and if you know a member of the family but not the deceased.

The letter need not be long, and it should be written as soon as possible after the death in question, ideally before the funeral. Appropriate sentiments might be 'I was very sad and shocked to hear of X's death. I never met him, but know how important he was to you. If there is anything I can do to help you at this unhappy time, please don't hesitate to ask.' Or '…he was always a good friend to me and I shall miss him enormously.' If you knew the person well enough to add a fond memory or an anecdote, so much the better: 'I shall always be grateful for his kindness when I was moving house and needed someone to look after my cat while I got settled' or 'I will never forget how tunelessly he sang "Happy Birthday to You" at my 21st' may make the recipient smile briefly and will show that you have put more than a little care and effort into your composition.

Old-style etiquette books say that it is inappropriate to send a card, rather than a letter, to express condolences. Her Ladyship is inclined to be more lenient, because in her view a card allows the sender to write fewer words and thus reduce his or her embarrassment. But she urges you to choose carefully: the flowery verses printed in some condolence cards may not be appropriate to those who took a robust view of this life and had no belief in any other. Nor does the fact that a card has a pre-printed message excuse you from writing a few words of your own. Even 'thinking of you at this sad time' is better than simply signing your name.

It is not necessary or appropriate to write a letter of thanks after a funeral, however generous the hospitality may have been.

Thank you

As with invitations, the formality of a thank you should match the formality of the occasion. A text to say 'Fab night, thanks xx' is fine after a casual supper with friends; it may not be acceptable to an older relative whose views are less up-to-date. Her Ladyship has an older friend who was much disgruntled when a beloved god-daughter merely texted her thanks for a substantial cheque sent for her sixteenth birthday. This reaction may have been old-fashioned, but it was heartfelt and the god-daughter (or perhaps her parents?) should have been sensitive to the likely reaction. A short letter that included the word 'generous' and a sentence such as 'It will take me a big step closer to that trip to New York' or 'I'm going to a wedding next month and now I shall be able to buy that smart new dress' would have taken ten minutes to compose and been well received.

As mentioned earlier, thanks for wedding presents should take the form of hand-written letters. So, too, should thanks for any extended hospitality, such as staying in someone else's home for more than a night or so. Remember that, in these days when the post rarely brings anything other than bills and junk, the pleasure of receiving a personal letter or postcard can far outweigh the effort that went into sending it. Never put a personal letter – particularly one of thanks, congratulation or condolence – through the office franking machine. It would be a shame to spoil the good impression writing a letter makes by indicating that you are too mean to pay for your own stamps.

It is a good rule of thumb for the young – in this context as in many others – to take into consideration the customs and attitudes of the older generation (however stuffy they may appear). It is also sensible for the older generation to realise that the young's values are different from those that prevailed a generation ago and that their casualness is not intended to be discourtesy.

Salutations and farewells

A hand-written letter (or a typed business one) should always begin 'Dear So-and-So'. The casual 'Hello' or 'Hi', or the omission of a greeting altogether, belongs in the world of email, and not always there (see below).

'Dear Sir or Madam' is used only in business letters if you don't know the name of the recipient; it is, to Her Ladyship's ear, decidedly cold in tone and likely to precede a complaint. 'Dear Mr/Mrs/Ms/Miss Fletcher' is the correct opening for business letters or if you are writing to an older person you don't know well.

'Dear Simon Fletcher (or Simone Fletcher)' cannot be described as elegant but is widely used for business letters when addressing the recipient as Mr or Mrs/Ms/Miss would be too formal.

'Dear Simon/Simone' should be reserved for friends and acquaintances, but may be used in both a work and a social context. In all but the most formal firms, once some sort of relationship is established it is usual to address someone by their first name even if you have 'met' them only by email or telephone.

Letters addressed to 'Dear Sir or Madam' should be signed 'Yours faithfully'; those to Mr or Mrs, 'Yours sincerely'. Whether you then add your given name or your initials is up to you, although obviously the former is more friendly; in either

Letters – the Royal Aspect

It is not usual to write direct to the monarch or senior members of the Royal Family: letters should be addressed to 'The Private Secretary to Her Majesty the Queen' or '…to His Royal Highness the Prince of Wales' and so on. The same applies if you wish to contact:

- the Royal Dukes (those of Edinburgh, Cambridge, York, Gloucester and Kent) and their Duchesses

- the Princesses Beatrice and Eugenie of York

- the Duchess of Cornwall

- Prince Harry of Wales

- the Earl and Countess of Wessex and their children

- the Princess Royal, Prince and Princess Michael of Kent and Princess Alexandra of Kent, but not their children

Non-royal dukes are addressed (on the envelope) as The Duke of X and at the beginning of the letter as 'Dear Duke'. Lesser members of the peerage are The Marquess of X, The Earl of X or The Viscount X. At the beginning of a letter to all these people, write 'Dear Lord X'. The wives of these peers, who are Marchionesses, Countesses and Viscountesses, are addressed as 'Lady X'. A life peer is The Lord X of Y and addressed as 'Lord X'; a life peeress is The Baroness X of Y and addressed as 'Lady X'.

With the exception of the eldest son, who usually uses his father's second title (the Marquess of Tavistock being the eldest son of the Duke of Bedford, for example), the offspring of dukes and marquesses are known as Lord James X or Lady Jemima X and addressed as Lord James or Lady Jemima. The eldest son of an earl is also a Viscount, but his siblings and the wives of his younger brothers are 'the Honourable', as is the eldest son of a Viscount; this is always abbreviated to 'the Hon.' on an envelope. In the body of the letter and in conversation, 'Honourable' is not used; holders of this title are addressed as Mr, Mrs or Miss.

case you should include your surname when closing a letter of this kind. Her Ladyship has one female friend who always signs business letters 'G A Malone' rather than 'Georgia Malone' because she feels that the recipient will assume that G A Malone is a man and therefore take the letter more seriously. Her Ladyship rather deplores the implicit sexism of this approach, but can't deny that it worked for the publishers of J K Rowling.

Her Ladyship rather deplores the implicit sexism of this approach, but can't deny that it worked for the publishers of J K Rowling.

If you address the recipient of your letter by their given name, you may sign off in any way you choose, from 'with best wishes' to 'lots of love', depending on the nature of your relationship.

Addressing envelopes

Envelopes containing personal letters should always be handwritten. Her Ladyship deplores the modern habit of using printed labels for Christmas cards, though she admits that in resisting this she is simply making the sending of cards more of a chore. But for a one-off letter, particularly of thanks or condolence, there is no excuse.

In formal correspondence to a Member of Parliament or a senior member of the judiciary or the church, use titles such as 'Rt Hon.', 'Right Reverend' and the like, and put 'MP', 'QC' and honours such as OM or CBE (but not university degrees or diplomas) after the name. It is still considered polite to address a man as 'Edward Cooper Esq' rather than 'Mr Edward Cooper', although this practice derives from an outdated piece of snobbery (only a tradesman was 'Mister') and is beginning to fall into disuse.

Telephones

Ever since email and text messaging were invented, they have been justified by the entirely reasonable claim that the recipient can deal with them at a convenient time. As these forms of communication have proliferated, telephoning out of the blue has come more and more to be seen as intrusive, particularly in the workplace. One friend of Her Ladyship, a busy chief executive, almost never receives or makes a call that hasn't been scheduled in advance.

Obviously ringing relatives and close friends for a chat remains a perfectly sociable thing to do. Many people ring parents or siblings every day and few are offended by a friend calling unexpectedly; explanations such as 'I was just thinking about you' or 'I realised we hadn't spoken for ages' are more likely to be flattering than not. But a ringing telephone has been likened to a badly behaved child saying, 'Talk to me now, talk to me now' and the caller should always been sensitive to the answerer's tone. If he or she sounds harassed or irritated, or has taken more than three or four rings to answer, it is always as well to ask, 'Is this a good moment?' The same applies if your conversation is likely to take some time: whether you want to discuss the provisions of your will or have a cosy gossip with an old friend, you don't want to feel that half her attention is being given to the children's bath water getting cold. If it *isn't* a good moment, the person receiving the call should offer to ring back at an appointed time: 'I'm in the middle of something – can I call you in half an hour?' or 'I'm going out in a minute – are you in tomorrow night?' are friendly and practical responses to an ill-timed call.

For similar reasons, it is impolite to ring at meal times and, unless you know someone's domestic habits well, before about nine o'clock in the morning or after nine at night. In a business context, don't ring anyone first thing in the morning on the day you know they have returned from holiday: give them a couple of hours to check their emails and go through their in-tray first. In pre-email days, when going on holiday meant you were genuinely out of touch for a fortnight, a friend of Her Ladyship had a client who was blithely indifferent to this rule: when the phone rang at 9.05 on her first morning back at work, she could guess who it was before she answered it, and she was always right. The client's behaviour was counter-productive in two ways: in the short term, she was unlikely to get an answer to her question – Her Ladyship's friend invariably had to say, 'I'm afraid I'm not up to date on that. May I call you back this afternoon?' In the longer term, it made the entire relationship more difficult, because Her Ladyship's friend took to thinking, 'Oh God, that'll be Monica' every time the phone rang early in the day and answered it with an inward groan.

If phoning abroad, be sure to calculate the time difference accurately. It is a source of constant amazement to Her Ladyship that if ever her telephone rings at three o'clock in the morning, it is a friend from California who hasn't realised what time it is in England; this is despite the fact that the parents of that friend live in Boston, so she has to be aware of time zones whenever she phones 'home'.

Be sensitive about bringing a phone conversation to an end. Whether or not you have initiated the call, there will come a time when you have said everything you have to say. At that stage it is perfectly polite to say, 'It's been lovely talking to you, but I need to get on with x, y or z.' If someone says that to you, don't start a new topic of conversation unless it is of paramount importance. To keep someone talking when they have expressed a desire to get away is simply rude. Her Ladyship has several friends whom she

Her Ladyship has several friends whom she never rings unless she has an hour to spare and has frequently had to invent excuses to end the conversation.

never rings unless she has an hour to spare and has frequently had to invent excuses to end the conversation. Another friend complains of a cousin who seems not to understand the words 'I have to go now.' After many years of frustration, the friend has perfected a technique of dealing with her garrulous cousin. She rings in the early evening and begins with the words, 'My dinner will be ready in twenty minutes, so I thought this might be a nice time to have a chat.' She then – whether it is needed or not – sets the kitchen timer to ring twenty minutes later and brings the conversation to an end. Drastic, perhaps, but sometimes a little tactful deceit is the only answer.

Leaving messages

Her Ladyship believes that if your call is answered by a machine or voicemail, you should always leave a message. Most modern telephones, both landline and mobile, record the fact that a call has been received from a certain number or numbers, and she finds it both frustrating and worrying to discover that someone has rung *without* leaving a message. What did they want? Was it bad news that they didn't want to entrust to a machine? Far better for the caller to say breezily, 'Nothing important. I'll try again later' than to leave the recipient in a state of anxiety.

On the other hand, messages should be brief and to the point. Leave your name and number if you think the person you are calling doesn't have it – and say it clearly and slowly enough for them to be able to write it down. Mention the time that you called and your reason for doing so, even if you are only ringing for a chat. The exception to this rule is truly bad news: it is more sensitive to say, 'Please ring me as soon as you can' than to leave a recorded message saying that someone has died.

Etiquette online

The advice never to write anything you would not care to see printed in a newspaper for all to read probably dates back to the invention of newspapers, and remains as sound as ever it was. It is even more important now that clicking a 'send' key can send a communication instantly, worldwide and, through the wonders of forwarding and 'favouriting', potentially to millions of people.

Email practicalities

Much of email etiquette refers primarily to the workplace, but its principles apply in private life too. They can be summarised as 'Be polite' and 'Don't waste people's time.'

In these days when everyone is notoriously busy, it is discourteous to bombard anyone with unnecessary emails. Help reduce the overload by giving your email an informative subject line, so that the recipient can judge how urgent it is, and by changing the heading if the substance of the message changes. It is sensible enough to head an email 'My complaint' if that is what your email is about; once the problem is solved, your fourth email may be to thank the person concerned. In that case it is only polite to remove the word 'complaint' from the subject line and substitute, perhaps, 'Thank you'. It is a lazy emailer who merely clicks 'reply' for the seventh time without bothering to ensure that the heading is still relevant.

Worse is the emailer who automatically 'replies to all', without considering whether their reply is relevant to all those who were copied in on the original message. If, for example, you email all the members of a group asking for a piece of information, one of them may reply positively (copying to the others to let them know that the matter is being dealt with).

Thereafter the correspondence should become one-to-one, between the person seeking the information and the person supplying it: there is no need to copy in everyone else. If you do, someone who has been away from their desk for a couple of hours may return to find a deluge of emails of which only the first two are of interest.

Avoid copying your boss in on every email you send. There is a difference between keeping him or her informed of important developments and trying to prove that you are doing your job. The latter smacks alarmingly of paranoia.

As for salutations, Her Ladyship's advice is to use them as you would in a letter (see page 143), with the exception that 'Hello' and even 'Hi' are permissible between friends and colleagues. A message with no greeting at all (unless it is in the middle of a trail of correspondence) is more like barking than talking.

When composing an email, the normal rules of writing apply: use full stops, capital letters and paragraphs when required. Her Ladyship has noticed with regret that she receives more and more emails that are brief to the point of terseness and end with a message along the lines of 'sent

Being able to deal with your emails while you are in transit is undeniably efficient, but it is no excuse for rudeness or sloppiness.

from my iPhone'. Being able to deal with your emails while you are in transit is undeniably efficient, but it is absolutely no excuse for rudeness or sloppiness.

Speaking of sloppiness, Her Ladyship urges you not to cut and paste text from the internet or another document straight into an email. It will be obvious this is what you have done, and give a bad impression. Format it in a Word document and copy and paste that. Always proof-read emails before you send them. Spellchecking is all very well, particularly for poor spellers, but nothing beats checking for yourself that you haven't typed 'there' when you mean 'their' or 'who's' when you mean 'whose'. Only if you are genuinely writing in a tearing hurry – you have been kidnapped by pirates, perhaps, attacked by bandits or your house is on fire – should you dispense with the courtesy due to the person who is going to read your email. Make it as easy, clear and relevant for them as you can.

Abusive language and rudeness of any form are as wrong in an email as they would be in a letter. Always remember that there is a human being on the receiving end and don't write anything that you wouldn't say to his or her face. A friend of Her Ladyship makes a point of telephoning anyone from whom she receives a terse or angry email. When she says, 'You seem to be angry; how can we sort this out?' the other person frequently responds apologetically and says, 'I didn't mean it.' Her Ladyship's view is: if you don't mean it, don't send it. By all means, if you are angry, type out a blistering email. It will make you feel a lot better. But save it as a draft, sleep on it (or at least go and have a cup of tea), edit it when you have cooled down and only then consider sending it.

The same friend has a rule that she applies to all office communications, and that works well in social situations too: if it is going to take more than three emails to resolve an issue, use the telephone instead. Even if you are doing something as apparently simple as making a lunch date, the 'I can't do Thursday, what about the following Tuesday?' 'Oh, no, I'm tied up on Tuesday' correspondence can go on indefinitely; pick up the phone with your diary in front of you (having fixed a time for the phone call if you think it is necessary) and the matter can be sorted in a trice.

Social networking

The common-sense rules that apply to emailing are just as important here (although the insistence on paragraphs and semi-colons can perhaps be relaxed). Never say anything on Twitter, Facebook or any other social site that you wouldn't say to someone's face; never post anything that you are going to be ashamed of in the morning (particularly a photograph that seems hilarious at the time); and always consider how you would feel if your remarks were quoted in a tabloid or *Private Eye*. Consider, too, how you would feel if someone said the same thing to or about you. If in doubt, don't do it.

Consider too how you would feel if someone said the same thing to or about you. If in doubt, don't do it.

Remember also that what is said cannot be unsaid; although a photograph misguidedly posted can be removed, it may already have been copied and may never be forgotten. A tweet may be only 140 characters but, carelessly or vindictively worded, it may still land you in court.

A CONCLUDING NOTE

While it is easy to dismiss the 'correct form' of yesteryear as quaint, there are occasions when 'classic' rules of behaviour are every bit as enduring as classic literature or classic cars. Lady Troubridge, whose wisdom has been quoted a number of times in the course of this book, included a section about travelling abroad, in which she warned her largely English readers against showing any feelings of superiority (this was the 1920s, remember). Expanding on the theme of 'when in Rome do as the Romans do', she observed:

> *Well-bred and polite people conform to foreign customs, no matter how strange and unusual they may appear. And they do it gracefully, with a smile of friendliness rather than one of disdain.*

Almost a hundred years later, Her Ladyship feels that 'a smile of friendliness rather than one of disdain' is still very much an attribute of the courteous person, at home or abroad and, as a general summing up of the precepts of this book, advises her readers to use it whenever they can.

FURTHER READING

Barnes, Jan, *Etiquette for Wine Lovers* (Copper Beech, 2001)

Bryant, Jo, *Debrett's A–Z of Modern Manners* (Debrett's, 2008)

Clayton, Nicholas, *A Butler's Guide to Table Manners* (National Trust, 2007)

Collins, Tim, *The Little Book of Twitter* (Michael O'Mara Books, 2009)

Gray, Lucy, *Her Ladyship's Guide to Modern Manners* (National Trust, 2006)

Morgan, John, *Debrett's New Guide to Etiquette and Modern Manners* (Headline, 1999)

Taggart, Caroline, *Her Ladyship's Guide to Running One's Home* (National Trust, 2012)

Taggart, Caroline, *Her Ladyship's Guide to the British Season* (National Trust, 2013)

Troubridge, Lady, *The Book of Etiquette* (Cedar Books, 1958; first published 1926)

Useful information also came from:

www.debretts.com

www.royalcollection.org

www.royal.gov.uk/royaleventsandceremonies/overview.aspx

www.hrstokes.com (Henry Stokes stationery)

www.telegraph.co.uk/technology/10287634/The-Debretts-guide-to-etiquette-in-the-digital-age.html

www.wikihow.com/Get-out-of-a-Car-Gracefully-Without-Showing-Your-Underwear

Index